My Pseudo-College Experience

www.mascotbooks.com

My Pseudo-College Experience

I have tried to recreate events, locales, and conversations from my memories of them. In order to maintain their anonymity in some instances I have changed the names of individuals and places. I may have changed some identifying characteristics and details such as physical properties, occupations, and places of residence.

For more information, please contact:
Mascot Books
620 Herndon Parkway, Suite 320
Herndon, VA 20170
info@mascotbooks.com

Library of Congress Control Number: 2020921399

CPSIA Code: PRV1220A
ISBN-13: 978-1-64543-842-7

Printed in the United States

DEDICATION

~

This book is dedicated to:

My mother, for planting this idea in my mind;

Tiffany DiMatteo, for teaching me how to love writing;

Emily Fillingham, for inspiring me to love to read;

Skyler, for supporting my goals and being honest always;

Sarah Eiley, for guiding me through doula work;

Alexis and Mikey, for giving me a community of love that felt like family;

Papa Crow, for recognizing my ambition, supporting it, and being my favorite person always;

Sophia, for teaching me to be a fighter;

Nancy, for calling me "Mighty Girl;"

Samuel, for pushing me to audit the class that led to this book becoming a reality and encouraging me to always chase what I want; and

Sergio and Martha, for being the ones who welcomed me into the Dartmouth community and helped me find my place on campus.

MY PSEUDO-COLLEGE EXPERIENCE

A MEMOIR

JESS KIMBALL

PREFACE

~

W hen you're sixteen years old, you're just trying to navigate college applications, Friday night football games, and SAT scores . . . well, most sixteen-year-olds. At sixteen, I was graduating and moving abroad, alone. I started a business, traveled, bought my dream car, moved into an apartment, then a tiny house, and then my first real house by nineteen.

Despite all those successes, I was constantly reminded that I still skipped a "vital" part of growing up: college. Now, don't get me wrong; I am very happy with my decision not to go and truly believe it is not meant for everyone. We should all follow our own paths, but regardless of how career driven and independent I was, I still longed to get a little insight into what all the hype was about. What exactly was happening in these frat basements that made people pine for school and refer to college as the "good ol' days?"

While running a business and expanding my company, I decided to add to my ever-so-busy schedule by auditing a class at an Ivy League college. Want the college experience? Visit a school in the middle of New Hampshire where we lack nightlife, and you'll definitely get it.

No students knew that I didn't actually go there until I told them; I was nineteen and appeared like any other college kid. I learned how to get into fraternities without an ID, where all the cool campus hangout spots were, and got an insight to the stresses these students were facing without actually facing them myself or having to pay a single dime.

My mom referred to me as a genius. I was getting the whole college experience minus the stress and financial burden, but are those aspects vital to the American college experience? How is the most stressful point in our young adult lives also the best time where we are "living it up" more than at any other point in our lives?

My college experience minus the debt and anxiety: *my pseudo-college experience.*

In a decade of creativity and unique career paths, is college necessary for all? Is the debt and stress worth it? Are you missing out if you choose a trade school or career path? Can you get the full college experience without actually attending?

I believe I did, and I did it Ivy League style.

I recall a moment when I told a friend about things I had experienced and he said, "I knew things like that happened, but I didn't know I knew someone they happened to." We all know someone who has experienced the events I did, they just don't talk about it. One of the things I can't stress enough after the experiences I have had is how much life needs to be talked about. If you look at me and think the things I discuss in this book are crazy, then you probably aren't the friend people feel they can turn to in tough times. Life is wild, beautiful, painful, and amazing all at the same time. People look at teens like they don't know what they are talking about, but the truth is, teens experience the pains of the world just as much as adults. The difference is that teens will question, because they can. When you turn eighteen you stop fighting so much and settle into adult life. You have to, you have responsibilities now. You push any pain and trauma out of mind because you need to keep moving, keep working to be able to live, to survive. My hope for those who read this book is that they will live a life they are proud of. They will keep questioning, keep fighting, and keep talking about the good, the bad, and the beautiful.

NO, I DIDN'T GO TO COLLEGE

~~

I graduated in December 2017. There was no ceremony until May, and I was not going to wait around for it. After all I had experienced in that town, I was ready to leave. I decided to pack up and move fourteen hours away from my family. It sounds kind of brave, like I'm full of independence, or maybe it sounds like I was running away. I chose to go somewhere I had family so I wouldn't be completely alone—the type of distant family you don't see often, but you would hope that they would come if an actual emergency occurred.

The truth is my high school experience was a bit of a mess. One semester into freshman year, I knew I didn't belong there. I came home on the bus crying to my mom that I couldn't do it anymore. I was quite exhausted from the undiagnosed OCD, depression, and just trying to figure out who I was. I was conforming to the mold of the perfect high school student, except that wasn't who I was, and everyone could see that. I was bullied for working so much, for who my family was, and for whatever I was interested in. I don't know how I got chosen as the one who would be picked apart; maybe they saw me as weak because I couldn't really handle it, if I'm being honest. I ended up transferring to an online school program. That was the moment everything changed.

I had the freedom to do whatever I wanted all day long. I'd bring my friends lunch at school and stay up late hanging out all night because I didn't have to be up early for school. Everyone seemed to like me again, but for the completely wrong reasons. I was being used for my car, my money, my freedom. I was lost, confused, and feeling slightly broken.

That broken feeling got even worse in my first semester of sophomore year because I was raped. It opened my eyes to who my real friends were and, honestly, I didn't have any. Everyone said I just couldn't handle rough sex and that I made it up. So, I transferred to a charter school and decided to reinvent myself. I was able to skip tenth grade and go straight into my junior year. I only had to do four semesters to graduate high school. I wanted to get out of there as quickly as possible because it wasn't long before everyone knew my past. They knew I was raped and that I handled that by hooking up with people. When the majority of the school body is Mormon or sheltered homeschool kids, someone who went through that sort of thing isn't really accepted. It brings out the dangerous people. A student harassed me online, leaving me feeling scared and completely alone. I only attended a third of classes and ate lunch alone in my car. My prom date cancelled a week before because he didn't think it was a good idea for us to be seen together after everything that had happened. At least, that's what his friends told me.

My last semester of high school, a student from my original school transferred in and we started hanging out. We went to visit her boyfriend at his college a few times. It was a great way to reaffirm my lack of desire to ever have a life partner or ever attend college. I was pushed to have sex with one of her boyfriend's friends, and then the next time we visited, I was kicked out of the dorm at 5 a.m. because the guy I slept with didn't like me. I drove back home in my friend's car and didn't tell anyone what happened. Shortly after, she told me she didn't want to ride home with her boyfriend because of some relationship drama. I drove the hour back to get her in a hurricane.

The truth is, when I was younger, no matter how much someone hurt me, I still went out of my way to help them. I was labeled the mom of the friend group and nicknamed "Mama Jess."

Maybe the reason I had a tiny sliver of desire to experience college life was because I wasn't allowed to party in high school. I went to plenty of parties, but people refused to let me drink because they forced me to be the designated driver. I felt like I couldn't just leave because they would all drive home drunk—I wasn't letting that happen. I was the person at the party who would stay up taking care of everyone and making pizza bagels for the hungry stoners at 4 a.m. The nickname of Mama Jess was funny, but it led me to process its origin and understand how to set boundaries in order to not be used by anyone in the future.

All these experiences contributed to the instant feeling of being lost and broken. I was more ready than ever to run for the hills when graduation came.

After a few weeks in New Hampshire, I realized I had no idea what I was doing with my life; what sixteen-year-old does? I had graduated as a certified doula, but choosing a trade school or certification career path means you are constantly reminded of its lack of stability. I wasn't at a point where doula work completely supported me financially, and I couldn't stand the daycare I was teaching in.

When I got a call to be an au pair in Paris, France, I went. The call happened to be from the doula who was at the first birth I ever attended. Her cousin lived in Paris and needed an au pair for her five children. This doula was someone I looked up to, a fierce mama of four with a house in the woods and a beautiful, massive garden, several animals, and a supporter of intentional communities (a community of people with different skill sets choosing to live together and support each other). I was grateful for her guidance in my birth work and for this Paris connection, so I went.

I didn't have the glamorous European experience most have. I was uncomfortable living with this family, and our differing political and religious beliefs resulted in what my therapist called an emotionally abusive and traumatic home life. The mother even brought over an American priest to try to help me with the painful experiences I had. The conversation consisted of him trying to convert me to Christianity and raving about my dad's big win in the 2016 Sweden UltraTri.

Not all moments were bad, though. One night, the mom and I were chatting about my life back in America. I talked about the women's circles I attended, and although she thought it was hippie-dippie nonsense, she showed me her idea of a girls' night. We bonded a little bit for the first time in two months while eating crepes and drinking wine. She told me I had a good brain and that it was impressive how I was able to understand where others came from.

It didn't make up for the children thinking I was evil, or being yelled at for not knowing how the buses in town worked, but it gave me something to hold on to—a memory that meant the trip was not completely bad.

I didn't have the confidence to go out and explore Paris because of all that was being said to me while living with this family. I spent my days walking the kids to school, sometimes stopping in the town bakery, and then sleeping the day away, extremely depressed. Those trips to the bakery felt like huge successes, but I barely recognized myself because of how sad I looked. I felt broken and terribly lost.

A weekend in London gave me a bit of a confidence boost and reminded me that I was capable of doing wonderful things on my own. There was a moment when my phone was dead and I was lost in the rain in central London. I couldn't find where I wanted to go, and I realized

I had brought the wrong adapter for my phone. I didn't have a way to charge it and was terrified. I anxiously sat in a Starbucks wondering what to do before eventually walking out, trusting things would work out as they should, and looking up to see the exact place I wanted to go directly in front of me.

I began to trust that the world wasn't so scary and things would happen as they were meant to. If I could accomplish everything I wanted to in the rain of London without a map and still make it to my host family's house two hours earlier than planned, I could easily pick a place to settle in my home country and chase my goals. My independent streak wasn't gone. I wasn't ruined, or that's what I kept telling myself, at least.

I returned to France, and things were just as bad as when I left for my weekend in London two days before. I knew I needed to return to the United States and stop forcing myself through this terrible situation. I returned still slightly lost, but with a new job and my first apartment just two weeks after that London trip.

I still felt like I had to settle in life. That family had drilled into my head that if I wanted to actually *be* anything, I needed the connections that college provided, but I still kept questioning it.

It seemed everyone who told me to go to school had a different reason why I should. Some said it would teach me to coexist with others, some said I would learn what I was passionate about, and others stressed the importance of the friendships made there.

I started working in a preschool before I decided to work in billing at a hospital. I thought it would offer me that security everyone spoke of. Paid time off, vacation time, insurance, a 401K, and tuition reimbursement . . . wow! I was set for life.

I began to settle. I continued my quirky life approach of going for what I wanted. I did photography on the side, baked, kept my Franceinspired wine snobbery going, and eventually decided to conceive a baby via donor sperm.

I decided that even though I chose to settle in my work life, I could still make the uncommon choice to have a baby on my own and eventually go to school with the help of tuition reimbursement. My time in France didn't crush all my dreams; I wouldn't let it.

Life felt okay. Some of my dreams were pushed to the back burner, but was being a doula really that practical? Security was being drilled into my brain, especially now that I was expecting a child.

My apartment felt safe. I had my little kitchen and an open floor plan to the living room. There was a small bedroom and a loft with a beautiful ladder leading up to it. It was the perfect first home. Things were starting to feel a bit more settled. I was happier than a few months prior. Things felt good, until . . .

Two months into my pregnancy, amongst all the chaos of life, I discovered I was having a miscarriage. Nothing like the biggest loss of your life thus far to make you question what you would do with your life going forward.

I packed up my dreamy New England apartment and moved back home. It didn't feel so dreamy anymore, and I felt completely shattered.

My dad began recommending ways to get me back on track. I swear, he was turning into a life coach. Taking some kind of class and getting a workout routine down were his solutions. To be fair, he never said it needed to be a college class. He said it could be crayon-making or hair-braiding if I wanted, just something to get me back on a schedule and caring about things again.

I explored real estate, nursing school (again), and accounting. No real interest was found in any of it. I always felt called back to that little certification I had for doula work. After a miscarriage, you really begin to understand why it takes a village to not just raise a baby but also exist.

I was still living with my parents, though, and I didn't feel whole just yet. I was in my childhood bedroom surrounded by everything from my apartment. I didn't feel completely okay. I felt lost.

I started hanging out with some people from high school again. The constant drama and immaturity resulted in many of those friendships ending, but some stuck, and they would last well into my future big moves. This was around the time I started going to parties for fun. One night my brother came to visit my parents, and I stayed with a friend in order to avoid the constant verbal abuse from my brother. This friend was throwing a party but didn't pressure me to be Mama Jess at all. In fact, I was spending the night, so I didn't have to worry about driving myself home. I was able to feel young and make up for the experiences I missed out on in high school. I didn't drink, but I got to just *be*, and that was something I didn't feel allowed to do before then.

I bet you're beginning to wonder why any of this is even important or relates to my decision to go to college, but stick with me here. The police showed up at this party, and they sat everyone down. Some people had jumped out of windows and run away, but the majority were listening to the cop's little speech. He asked who had plans to go to college. Everyone except me raised their hand. Every single person, though I can almost guarantee some of them didn't want to actually go. He explained that if he arrested everyone for drinking, they would no longer be accepted by the colleges they had planned on going to. I began to understand just how hard it can be for some people to attend the schools they wanted. The exclusivity angered me, and again I found myself really not liking the college process. You apply to schools, pay fees, wait, experience intense stress, and then possibly have a moment of excitement if you were accepted before you return to the stress of financial aid, student loans, scholarships, and debt. That little party experience was enough to have me focusing on work again.

I relaunched my business, focused on postpartum support, and started traveling again. When I did that, I felt things slowly begin to be okay again.

It was during my time in Hawaii that I really felt called to do more. Things began falling into place just after that relaunch, and I felt completely set in my choice to be a doula. Of course, many still felt the need to recommend other schooling options to me, but I had the confidence to just smile and nod. I knew I was doing what I was meant to.

Hawaii was a very transformative experience. I became friends with a group that completely misjudged who I am as a human being. They viewed me as stuck up, using people to get what I wanted, and not understanding of hardship. That broken feeling just seemed to never want to go away.

I ended those friendships and decided to focus completely on myself. I went to my favorite seawall one day to journal and watch the sunset. I was there to focus on myself, but all I could focus on was the cute boy next to me. I overheard a woman describe him as polite and handsome, so I looked over to see just how handsome he really was. He wasn't there, though, he was in front of me waving me over. I pointed at myself and said, "Me?" He nodded, so I went over. He was showing me sea turtles and had me take pictures of them. It was nice to have a new friend on the island.

He gave me his name and number, telling me to remember him because one day he would be a published author. I texted him, but no response. The next day, I sat on the seawall coloring in my journal and listening to music, looking up every so often, wondering if he would be there. I told myself to not be so obsessive and focus on my journal, until I saw feet walking towards me. I looked up, and he smiled and said, "Hi, stranger." His phone had broken, and he felt bad I couldn't reach him, so he looked for me where we met—that seawall where I sat every day.

We explored the island, visited markets, ate amazing food, and got to know each other more and more. Every moment I wasn't working, I tried to spend time with him. I didn't tell him any of my traumas. I felt free. We met in the evenings at the secret beach I found and called Turtle Cove. We had sex on the beach, and for the first time in my life I cared about a boy. It was pure lust—something I had never experienced before. He was flirty, smart, funny, and had this strange level of control over me. It was all a bit hypnotic. The way he made me feel was just *wow*.

But then he left. He went back to Oklahoma, and I spent my last two weeks in Hawaii exploring and enjoying my time there, texting with him and FaceTiming all day . . . not yet aware he was a liar. I told him how much I missed him, and he became distant as he began to feel the lies catch up with him. Once I was back in the Carolinas, my friend stalked his social media and discovered the lies. I felt sad for him. How sad does your life have to be for you to feel the need to make up such big lies about it? But was I any better by not mentioning all the trauma I had been through?

My third miscarriage was just after this. I'd have four of them by nineteen, no matter what birth control I was on, where I was at in my cycle, or what precautions we both took. I kept getting pregnant but couldn't carry the pregnancy to term.

My mom, over time, became extremely supportive and in awe of my ability to create a successful business. I still am unsure of my dad's true opinion, but he seems to support the decision I made. My grandfather called me the only real "businessman" of the family and expressed pride and admiration for what I had accomplished.

My relationship with my parents wasn't great, even when they became more supportive. Shortly after my return from Hawaii, I went on a date with someone eight years older than me, and he raped me. I was in denial of this happening again, and my relationship with my parents became more strained. This led to me not dating for a while. Between the miscarriages and the rape, I wanted nothing to do with men. I moved in with my best friend's family for a while and distracted myself with work.

Eventually, I relocated back to the New Hampshire area. I was known just as a doula, not Mama Jess or the girl that couldn't handle rough sex or the girl who couldn't stop getting pregnant and miscarrying. I offered new kinds of services to the area I was in. Nobody knew of the messy years I had just experienced. My first day in that town, I knew I had to stay there. I called my mom and said, "For the first time in my life, I feel like I can breathe. I am not coming home."

I had this odd feeling something great was waiting for me inside the college in that town, but I knew it wasn't enrollment. I discovered my great grandfather went to that school and soon learned it was Dartmouth College. I was set on teaching there one day—but was determined to accomplish that with no degree.

I returned to my parents' home in South Carolina for three weeks to finish out a contract and convert a vintage camper into my tiny house. It was a purple vintage Frolic with yellow trim. It was very small, but my dad built a wonderful new bed with tons of storage, and I added a table and beautiful antique peacock chair. I had a tiny vintage-style kitchen and a small bathroom-closet combo. It had character and was a unique way to live. I was excited for life's new adventure and all the odd experiences it would allow me to have.

My dog and I headed back north and lived a busy life of preschool teaching, hiking, doula-ing, and lots of puppy snuggling in our home in the woods, surrounded by beautiful Vermont's beauty, only twenty minutes from my workplace.

Things felt like a movie, like those pinch-me moments that people sometimes describe. Those dreamlike moments rarely happen, but I think we should strive to have at least one every day. When life is going better than you can comprehend, when you're surrounded by wonderful people who make you feel light, when you begin to feel your heart go soft, those are the moments that make you say, "Pinch me, I must be dreaming."

Life wasn't always sunshine and rainbows, though. I had more miscarriages, struggled to have any kind of positive relationship with my family, and grieved the loss of my grandmother and the loss of my kitten. The struggle to find other young professionals to socialize with was hard to navigate, and I kept trying to avoid the college in order to separate myself from those young community members.

Not too long after moving to the area, I ended up moving my tiny house onto a new friend's property . . . a very risky decision in the event that we stopped getting along, but I wanted to take the chance. That friend? She had a baby and was married to a Dartmouth student. Throughout this friendship, I watched my friend birth her second baby, open her childcare center, and buy her first home all by the age of twenty-three. She brought out wonderful, positive characteristics in me, made me question life's meaning, and encouraged my growth. All I can hope is that I encouraged the same in her.

My goal to avoid campus was quickly unmet when I started getting introduced to her and her husband's friends. Now, I'll admit that I was wrong: these students are hardworking, great people whom I am glad to have met. I even found myself considering applying to go to school there. I eventually decided to attend community college instead, but despite being financially independent for three years, living alone, paying all my bills, and not really speaking to my parents much after all the traumas I experienced in my teen years, I still didn't qualify as an independent. The requirements to claim yourself as an independent opened my eyes to the exclusivity that affects every college, not just the Ivies—something I discovered was very specific to America. I realized how problematic tuition and student loans really are. For these reasons, I decided not to attend community college. It just wasn't a practical choice because of the debt. You can help one person by doing something like anonymously paying their tuition, something I witnessed a family do, and it's an amazing thing, but it only helps one person. I wanted to change in the way these schools operated, but first I wanted to fully understand it.

My friend and I bonded over babies and being young entrepreneurs. She supported my decision to start going onto campus, and we laughed over wine and pizza about the experiences I had afterwards. Then I would retreat to my tiny house and do it all again the next day.

Her husband became a big-brother figure to me, and these two random friends whom I had met through a Facebook group were quickly family. He was the first person to give me a tour of Dartmouth campus. We met up during my lunch break, and he showed me a few spots he frequented. We finished the tour with him taking a photo of me in front of Baker Library—my first photo on campus. The safe space that is so important to have in everyday life, but can be hard to find when you move somewhere new, was discovered for me in their welcoming home. Although not every one of my choices had their support, I could trust them to give me their honest opinion, step in if things got out of hand, and be there for me to lean on the way family is. They didn't ever push me to go back to school and accepted my ambitions, even when they seemed a bit out there.

I noticed that when people learned how often I worked and what I made yearly doing postpartum support they would stop pushing me to do something new or go to school. My car became this symbol of my success that started to shut people up. It was strange to me because my idea of success didn't involve income, but if what you were doing made you happy.

One of the students referred to me as a "scammy witch," and I realized that many people would recognize my successes but be angered by them. I was heartbroken. All I had worked for got me dubbed a scam artist, when these trust-fund babies were using their parents' connections and money to go to an Ivy League school. Not cool. I was turned off college students again and was prepared to avoid them altogether. Like I said, I'm not one to put myself in situations that don't bring me joy if I don't have to.

While all of this was happening, two new people moved into my friends' house: a Dartmouth graduate and a Dartmouth sophomore. That graduate student became an amazing support person for me. He listened to me cry about not knowing what to do with my life, how to navigate this college thing, and what was happening in my relationships. Looking back, I put him through way too many tear-filled rants, but he provided me with much-needed advice and supported me during an intense, transformative time. I am forever grateful for him showing me KAF (King Arthur Flour, a great bakery) for the first time and giving me a tiny bit of confidence to get back out there.

A pre-med student I was becoming friends with recommended I audit a sociology class. I had been toying with the idea of auditing but had no success in getting a response from a professor. Well, this class's professor responded in a timely fashion, and I was set to audit the class the following month. I was going to give "being friends with college students" one more shot.

I found myself extremely nervous, wondering what students would think of my car or tattoos or the fact that I didn't really go there. Most of them didn't notice I wasn't a student, and the ones who did notice seemed to find it interesting. Blending in wasn't too hard since I had a friend to sit with, though it felt like high school that first day when I didn't know where to sit in the lunchroom.

I was grateful for the friendships I was beginning to really form. As I began spending more time with students outside of my regular friendship group and frequenting campus almost daily, I discovered myself feeling like a college student and experiencing the social life of one without actually attending—all the education, cafeteria food, frat parties, and social stigmas without actually going to college. My pseudo-college experience had begun.

THE GOOD OL' DAYS

I constantly hear college referred to as the "good ol' days"—the peak of one's young adult life, the greatest memories you'll ever make. Think about that just a little. The moments spent blacked out on a fraternity basement floor are the moments you are going to long for years later? When you have a partner or your dream job or reach whatever bucket-list goal you set for yourself, you'll still pine for Saturdays with the boys?

This is something that really scared me. I couldn't comprehend how I could experience the Eiffel Tower and Hawaii beaches or fall in love in the streets of Athens after midnight but still be told that the greatest high I'd feel in life would be in a fraternity. How could that be the advice these wise, older people needed to bestow?

Growing up, adults would give me advice relating to choosing a major or seeing the world and finding love, but once it was discovered that my lack of interest in attending college wasn't just a gap year or two, they shifted their advice to drinking habits and the careless friendships that they felt "stood the test of time."

Honestly, the friendships that have lasted the longest in my life are ones with people I met thousands of miles from my home. The first boy I ever loved was the one I met on my favorite seawall in Kona. The moment I knew I chose the right career was when a conservative French politician told me I hadn't. The stories I heard and memories I made in the first few years post high school were ones that shaped who I am today in ways college never could have. I can't imagine being the person who peaked in high school or college. Watching someone in their sixties grasp onto those experiences and never fully let go of the fact that they are over is something that scared me deeply, especially with two out of three Americans regretting their degree choice or going to school at all. It is my desire to make every day feel so amazing that I can't believe it's real. I think I'm one of the lucky ones to believe what I believe so deeply that I always follow the path I want, despite caring about others' opinions.

We tend to crush the not-so traditional dreams children have once they are old enough to understand. We drill practicality into their minds and get rid of imagination, telling them imagination is for play, not reality. There is a secure path you are meant to follow for all to be safe and well. How practical is that path with gender and racial bias? With the high financial burdens of student loans? The overly competitive job market? The golden trophy of health insurance seems to be the main reason people feel called to this path. They know from a very young age that we are not provided any real security and that life is a constant fight, even if the fights differ according to income level.

Do you really want to be in your sixties recalling the good ol' days? Will health insurance make it all worth it? What do you see as a priority in your life? Go and make life feel a little dreamier!

DARTMOUTH

~

This campus is one of the best campuses in the United States. It's obvious when you read articles like "Dartmouth Frats Ranked by Architecture." Not every school could publish that and actually get people excited about reading it. It was voted the prettiest of the Ivy League schools, and the town of Dartmouth encompasses the classic Hallmark lifestyle. There's an incredible walkability with a beautiful inn in town, eateries, gelato, a movie theater, live music at The Skinny Pancake crêperie, and adorable shops for whatever you need. The stores cater to sorority girls and preps, stocked full of the trendiest, tiniest dresses and tops, all incredibly overpriced.

Families crowd the green enjoying picnics and games of frisbee. Young teens play guitar in an effort to impress. You can walk to the bakery and enjoy a fresh fruit tart or run errands at the co-op.

You will feel like you're in a storybook town with the cobblestone paths and adorable trendy coffee shops. Just watch out for students if you're driving. They don't look before crossing the street; the first sign of their sense of entitlement.

The movie *Animal House* is based on a Dartmouth fraternity, Alpha Delta. This is the fraternity that lost Dartmouth recognition for branding members with hot pokers on their asses. Everything came crashing down when one sophomore's branding got infected. This wasn't the first time this fraternity had been suspended, and even though this all went down four and a half years prior to my time at Dartmouth, it still was a hot topic of discussion. After a certain book came out and the "modern war on frats" began, students never really let it go. You have the groups of students that believe they were rightfully closed and the groups that think it's "all fun and games," but it's only fun and games until someone gets hurt. You'll witness a lot of people getting hurt.

The movie shows the fraternity members engaging in drunken behavior and having frequent encounters with administration, which was not that far off from the reality of the AD fraternity.

Don't be scared of Greek life (the fraternity and sorority lifestyle) just because of news stories and books like *Confessions of an Ivy League Frat Boy* by Andrew Lohse. That title is a mouthful, and the book itself is an exaggeration of events happening on campus, lacking the real fun you will experience, which does not involve coke—trust me on that one. You probably won't even see any drug use on campus, let alone in the town of Hanover.

The frat party addiction is not because of drugs or alcohol. It comes from the high you get from being around people who only have one concern: having a care-free evening. When attending such an academically demanding school, you need those types of nights.

You'll wonder why the other students doing coke in the story Lohse wrote didn't lose their shit and blame the entire university for their reckless decisions. Why didn't they also assault campus security with a chair?

Yes, you will be concerned about entering frat parties alone with the handsy guys and possible hazing gone wrong, but not to the extent that this book makes you feel you should.

FRAT PARTIES ARE FOR FOOLS AND ALCOHOLICS

~

T hings have changed a bit since the times of *Confessions of an Ivy League Frat Boy*. Rules are stricter, and frats have been shut down. The modern war on frats changed the scene quite a bit, but that doesn't mean all the craziness is gone. The fun is just less harmful, like hiding hot dogs all over the fraternity for members to find or covering someone's car with condoms and tampons. If you're looking for a particularly gross prank, try hiding fish in the vents of the frat house or on the balconies.

You never witness or hear of the hazing you read about in news articles. The frats really aren't as scary as people make them out to be. Of course, there are some nerves during your first frat party, just not as much as you expected. You walk up to the door of a fraternity. You've never been to one, and you're alone. It's a whole other kind of terrifying. You realize the door is locked. Why were you so confident? Were you just going to waltz right in? You don't own the place. When you enter, someone goes to ask you for your ID, but before they can even finish their question, you quickly say, "I'm meeting someone." You don't look at them and won't be able to ever recall who they were.

This experience stays with you forever. It's the time you learned how to get into a frat party without an ID. That flash of a Tinder profile and three simple words is all it takes.

You begin to take in the setting you've entered. There is a not-so-obvious theme going on. Random decor hung throughout the house. People are in Hawaiian shirts and tie-dye pants. You won't ever discover what the theme actually is. You finally find a face you recognize, and the tour of the house begins.

The first place you go is down to the basement. You start to feel your Doc Martens sticking to the floor. At this point, you don't know if this is a common occurrence and just make a mental note to wear a less bulky shoe next time. You'll later learn that slip-ons aren't a good choice either because the sticky beer-covered floor will pull the shoe right off your foot.

The basement doesn't give off the classic American movie depiction of fraternities you thought you'd witness. There are people scattered about playing pong . . . the special Dartmouth kind of pong. (Dartmouth pong is different from normal beer pong. It's played with paddles that don't have handles. The legend is that men were so angry when women came to Dartmouth that they broke the handles off so women couldn't hold the paddles. You know, 'cause our dainty little hands aren't big enough to hold the paddle without handles.)

You are trying to be a fly on the wall and not stand out more than you already have in your lack of theme-appropriate attire, so you decline playing and follow your friend around instead. He enters a room at the back of the basement. You casually enter along with him and quickly learn that this room is only for frat members and you can't legally be in there. He grabs a drink, and you both exit. That room doesn't have much in it, just an empty metal shelving unit and a plain white fridge that's oddly placed a foot from the wall instead of against it.

You'll soon learn about the floor situation and hear the story of the monthly pressure washing that must be done to deal with the sweat, puke, and alcohol that causes the sticky coating on the cement. One fraternity contains a trough for people to empty all their bodily fluids into, a trough that drains into a corner of the room, keeping the stickiness contained.

The two of you head upstairs. The rooms are not what you imagined, either. You enter a room that doesn't belong to him. The walls are covered in Renaissance paintings of naked women, and there is a guy in the corner of the room, his friend. He is a redhead "jokingly" making excuses for any guy that insults a girl during a pick-up line. His words reek of toxic masculinity.

You enter a door at the back of the room that leads to his room. Both rooms are very small, but this one is more of a closet. It is definitely just a closet.

You decide to go see a bit more of the house and head to another room. You are quickly greeted by a student from the class you're auditing and start talking. You start making up inside jokes and end up messaging him later to ask about a class assignment. That message sparks an unexpected friendship.

The room this meeting is taking place in is slightly bigger and has about ten people in it. There is a small disco ball that covers the ceiling in a multicolored light show. The TV is set to a video playing on loop of a kaleidoscopic animation. Everyone is sitting, silently vibing to the music and drinking punch.

You are shocked at first when you see the punch being scooped out of a trash can but learn this is common house-party practice. You are reminded of the experiences you had at parties in high school when you would just sit around a fire or in a living room, everyone silent, just drinking from a solo cup and zoning out. The lack of excitement gives you those "this is cool because no parents are around to stop it" vibe.

Look up, and you'll notice a sock covering the smoke detector to block the sensor so that members can smoke in their rooms. You wonder how they didn't learn their lesson when, just the week before, firetrucks showed up at the same fraternity to deal with a bong that had caught fire in a bedroom.

You are quickly swept away—scratch that. You are *pushed* down a staircase, as fraternity members rush to a brother's aid as he stumbles out of the bathroom wearing only a towel and then completely blacks out. You are told to ignore everything you saw and never speak of it again. You'll never learn what was wrong with the guy, but you hope he was all right.

You end up back in the trippy TV room again. It's a lot of walking around the fraternity, going from room to room. This second trip to the room is a little more exciting than the first. You run into someone you know from your sociology class. This sparks one of the first friendships you'll have on campus. Despite all the strangeness you experience in the fraternity that night, something good will come from it.

Next you are headed up to the president's room, but not before you take a bathroom break. Big mistake. The bathroom is a wreck. Something even having four brothers could never prepare you for. The floor is wet from the sinks and, presumably, urine. There is poop smeared in some stalls, and all the seats are up. The trash cans are all overflowing, and the soap and paper towel dispensers are all empty.

You try to ignore the experience you just had and head upstairs. The room you enter has a select few people in it and they're spread out on couches. They're all very welcoming and ask you about your life. They seem interested, but it isn't until you mention you're a "legacy" that they really get excited. You throw this fact around a lot, and it annoys your friends, but how cool is it knowing you moved to a town and discovered after the fact that your great-grandfather lived there when he was your age and—cooler still—happened to be a member of the same fraternity that you're now in nearly a hundred years ago? Everyone in the room, except your friend, will get overly excited by this fact and insist you go looking for pictures of great-grandad on the wall of presidents later. This is the moment you will learn just how convenient being a legacy is when it comes to getting into places on campus that are slightly restricted.

Eventually, you head back to your friend's closet of a bedroom and listen to music, just sort of vibing, before a period emergency occurs. Blood everywhere, like someone was murdered type of thing. He doesn't care, though, and tells you to spend the night if you need to; he'll wash the sheets in the morning. He offers to run, literally run, down the street to CVS to grab tampons. All you can think about is how Phi Tau is directly across the street and has plenty of tampons in the bathroom. You just ignore the blood and hang out longer (murder scene was probably an exaggeration).

He goes searching for tampons after a few minutes because he wants you to feel comfortable staying over. He asks people all over the house if they have any. They give him an odd look, eye the massive hickey on his neck, and ignore him, so he returns feeling defeated.

He ends up leaving the room for what he says will be five minutes. Thirty minutes later, he returns on some kind of drugs. He has other people with him, and they walk in on you basically half asleep. They keep asking if you're okay and you insist you need to head home. They keep trying to give you water, assuming you had too much to drink and realizing that you are ready for bed by 3 a.m. When you finally leave, all you get is a goodbye fist bump and a "drive safe" before everyone heads back to their partying and you drive home in your bloody pants. Luckily, nobody can see the blood.

You'll notice the trust between the brothers is strong and that they protect each other regardless of how big the mistake one of them made is. When the COVID-19 pandemic hits and campus is locked down, you'll begin seeing that trust unravel. The parties that continue on campus during the pandemic are supposed to be top secret, but someone told someone and that someone, tells you and quickly you, are hearing about it from every frat-party goer you know. Seeing the brothers stop trusting each other will give you a very different view of fraternity life.

The more you frequent frat row, you'll find yourself noticing differences between each frat. The term "milk and cookies frat" is something you hear often. You assume it's some kind of slang term for the fraternity that doesn't allow alcoholic parties. Turns out, it's not. It's a quarterly party where a certain fraternity has all its members bake two kinds of cookies and everyone is welcome to come try them and vote on the best. So many cookies are left over you get invited back to fill a Tupperware container the next day in an effort to clear out some of the food.

A lot of students don't know about this event or don't go because it isn't that popular, but it is kind of the perfect activity for a Friday night. What do you want after participating in recreational activities? Food. What does this party have? Too much food. Take your Tupperware container, fill it up, and then get stoned. This recommendation will get you a lot of respect on campus.

Events like this are something you would love to invite your best friend to. Wholesome nights with cookies and ice cream are a great way to introduce someone to the frat-party scene if they've never been to one before. That's a little hard when your friend is six months pregnant, though. She'll probably just have to live vicariously through your stories instead. It's a weird time in your twenties, when half your friends are married with kids, and the other half are blacking out in frat basements on the regular.

During this experience you'll learn that Dartmouth students can't cook. This creates the ongoing joke you have that "Dartmouth students can't make toast." Just ask them, they can't, and the ones who can make toast do it in some bizarre way, like in an oven. They can't use an actual toaster because they either had a chef that used an oven or a nanny that never taught them how to prepare toast. One of the trays of food at the party will always be referred to as the "cancer food" because a student had baked the food on the plastic tray. Just walk behind Phi Tau, and you'll find a pile of trays that have been thrown out each time this has happened. This fraternity also has students that don't add water to boxed macaroni and cheese and who forget to turn off the water when refilling their humidifiers so water leaks into a ceiling light downstairs and causes water damage. You aren't even shocked when you hear the story of the student who didn't know how to make microwave popcorn and put it in for a full five minutes, even when it was burning. How could anyone be shocked by that story after seeing all those other events before?

These students are the future leaders of industry and science, but the majority don't understand how the world works because they have experienced extreme levels of privilege. They all feel they greatly deserve to be there, even though some are only there because of who their parents are. The students who really worked and fought to get in don't get any recognition for it, especially when the school worships athletics over academics. They tend to be smart in a specific subject, the thing for which they enrolled, but outside of that subject, they're a bit clueless. If they grew up in a rural or more remote area, they don't have much exposure to real-world problems that occur in bigger cities, like Chicago or West Philadelphia. They may be witness to some sort of poverty in their town, but they won't understand some of the political issues happening in the present day. Thankfully, you'll notice some of those students getting educated on these issues in classes like your health disparities class. It's an interesting outcome, the human being that grew up in a place like Los Angeles and saw the poverty and discrimination some faced but didn't have to experience it themselves because they were white and born into a high-income household. The separation between the group they join and other groups sticks with them into high school, and you think it'll disappear at college, but you end up surprised because students of color stick together in the dining hall and the athletes still get their own section that seems to be a bit better than all others. Of course, you aren't shocked when international students stick together because they have a shared experience, but it is sad to think that students of color bond over the experience of being treated differently, not the homesickness they feel for their home country or culture, like international students do.

The same fraternity that doesn't know what tray goes in the oven is also the one that engages in SEX. The "Sunday Evening Xtravaganza" is an ice cream social for anyone who wishes to attend held every weekend. Learning all of the best food spots is a great secret power to try to develop.

It also happens to be the fraternity where you first learned how to play pong. You scored on maybe two shots? Pong isn't really your thing, but it was like an initiation into Dartmouth culture. You ignored the hard liquor ban on campus and took two shots of vodka. Your playing seemed to improve after that. There weren't many people there, with it being the start of break—just you, your sociology class friend, and two people you didn't know. They ended up being two of the funniest people you met on campus and you enjoyed walking around with them shivering in the cold as you headed to Collis for your first meal on campus. It was late, so you just got a smoothie, but you learned about all the wonderful food options in just one of the campus dining locations.

The more you frequent campus, the more often you get invited to events. It's your birthday, and an acquaintance invites you to a fraternity party. You're excited. I mean, it is your birthday, it's your night, and you want to live it up. It takes you a while to find the frat house; it isn't on frat row. The fraternity has a beautiful trans flag on it, and you are quickly welcomed in by someone. Everyone is dressed as a fairy. You have that feeling of being so tired you don't really know what is real. Everyone begins introducing themselves and makes sure to tell you their pronouns. People are bonding over their zodiac signs and enjoying laughter-filled conversations. This fraternity is another co-ed and primarily houses members of the LGBTQ community. You feel like you have entered a safe haven. All of those stereotypes on campus can't touch you here. People invite you to play pong and dance around the house.

That fraternity will be the biggest contrast you see to the football fraternity. The football frat is the most popular when it comes to "tails nights," parties starting around ten at a fraternity attended by one or more sororities. Getting the players attention isn't that hard, but getting to one of them is difficult. The basement is packed, so good luck ever trying to play a game of pong there. You can barely move through the room, and you constantly feel people brushing up against you. You can't tell if they're touching you on purpose or accidentally while trying to walk past. It's hard to feel safe when an unwanted guy is hitting on you or when you're lost in the crowd.

The football players aren't that bad. They're all decent, smart, and pretty considerate. They seem to have each other's backs and spend time in a pack. But you'll find the classic frat boys in the hockey frat—those ones who make you laugh a little because they all dress the same and spend all day drunk. The best story you'll hear? The one about the hockey frat's ice rink party. You hear about "skates and sluts" way after the fact because it was such a fail. You hear about how the boys filled their basement with water and opened all the windows to get it to freeze. The floors were so damaged that the hockey boys lived in alternative housing options while construction was done. This creates one of those stereotypes, so every time you hear someone say they play hockey, you just laugh. You wonder what those students will do while not living together because the only reason they pass classes is they all take the same courses and use the "test banks" in the basement, which were described to you as filing cabinets. At least the guys are organized.

There are many different kinds of frat boy. You take a drive down frat row to see what they do during daylight hours. They don't look up at your car unless you have some kind of rap or trap music playing—another way you end up making friends on campus.

One thing you notice happening often is girls stealing things from fraternities: stealing a pot from a kitchen to make spaghetti in her dorm, stealing fraternity doors, mattresses, photos, decorations, or all the T-shirts in the laundry room. The one you'll find funniest is food theft. It seems like the lamest thing to steal unless you're super hungry, but the boys will throw temper tantrums over food. One girl stole Oreos and a member punched a hole in the wall. Another ate all the pizza but pulled all the pineapple off and left it next to the passed-out member. They ended up getting married, so all seems to be forgiven.

You can spot the diversity during this short one-street drive. Some fraternities have minivans and pickup trucks parked outside and broken barbecue grills littering the street. Another frat might have a clean lawn and a rainbow flag hanging out front, and this one makes you smile slightly because the most common frat-yard look features the classic broken TV out front, random couches and futons on the front porch, and a grill out front.

The fraternity stereotype is so well known it even gets brought into class curriculum. In a lesson on gender disparities, one of the main topics will be about the way different genders act on campus. The frat boys are known for showing off and taking up as much space as they want, while other campus members tuck themselves away in their corners of the library or dining hall or wherever they are. You believe the guys mean well because it's 2020 and they're trying to treat others as equals, but society has not done enough to end their subconscious sexist behavior.

The frat parties allow you to have a little insight to the members' creative sides. Their ability to decorate or come up with a cool theme is funny to watch. With COVID-19 going on, you'll find yourself joking about corona-themed frat parties years from now with Corona-brand beer, masks being worn, and a bit of an apocalyptic vibe going on. Party like it's 2020, right?

That's what the students are doing. Despite the pandemic, many students choose to return to campus. Whether it's because of a tough home life, missing their significant other, or just missing frat life, they're back. You see couples having picnics on the green again, frat boys hanging outside Collis working on laptops, international students studying (you don't know what because you aren't multilingual. What is it about people speaking a foreign language that makes them so much more attractive?). You even see students running the campus food truck again and stop by for some Mediterranean yumminess.

The frat scene is such a big deal on campus that nobody wants to be stuck in their dorm room on a Wednesday night, when the all-night parties are happening. Of course, social media is huge in 2020, so you can expect to find all the big party moments posted on Instagram—so many posts that it gets to the point where you can match up different people's pictures and see the entire room they were in. You'll find multiple photos of the exact same moment taken at the exact same second from different angles. It's like you're actually there, so don't feel bad about staying in to study. The dorms will be quiet, and nobody will know you missed the party because you can talk about exactly what happened just from the information you gathered on social media posts.

If you want the college frat experience, but aren't a student, you can actually join a frat. Dartmouth has a co-ed fraternity that anyone could join. You would have to pay fees, like students, and you could only live there in the summer, but you would still have a frat experience. Just go sign their rush book.

Frat life may not be for everyone, though. Just a mere two-thirds of students, not everyone. Some don't even know what it is. When your best friend's husband was asked about Greek life, he just imagined weird toga parties and was confused. He wasn't far off, though. There definitely are toga parties. Students will wear a bedsheet and sandals. The parties became even more common after their appearance in *Animal House*.

DON'T BRING THE BABY TO KAF

One of the turn-offs to going back to school after years away from that setting was all that you went through. After traveling the world, experiencing pregnancy losses, and finding love, you didn't think you would be understood. Most nineteen-year-olds don't know what it's like to have a miscarriage or experience a pregnancy. You think about hiding what you experienced, but it's such a big part of who you are. The experiences shaped you into the driven, ambitious, strong person you are today. You wonder about the young parents attending school. Do they feel like they have to hide the fact that they have a kid?

One day, a past doula client reaches out to see if you'd do them a favor and nanny for a few months. One of the best parts of this nanny job was that you could bring the baby out and about on campus. Her dad took care of her while you were in class, and the rest of the day, you were either at her home or out showing her the world. You quickly picked up on the constant stares while on campus. You'll eventually learn to just stare back. You want to provoke people to get them to say what they're thinking.

You're in the library, meeting a friend for coffee. You have the baby with you and decided to meet at KAF, the King Arthur Flour location in Baker Library. You two are talking, baby is laughing, and you're splitting a muffin with her. You can't help but get distracted by the staring. You always thought you would be a chill parent once you had kids, but this day in the library you learned that wasn't the case. You notice a girl from across the room taking Snapchats of you and the baby. You immediately feel the need to go confront her, but your friend calms you down. You focus back on the conversation at hand.

Moments later, a group sits down at a table just a few feet away. You notice them eying you and, again, you're distracted. You eventually mouth, "What?" and they speak up. They want to know how old the baby was. You answer, and one says to another, "I told you she wasn't a freshman." You awkwardly laugh and spend the rest of your coffee meeting focused on the conversation, but slightly uncomfortable. You begin to understand why some parents don't feel confident bringing their babies out, especially young parents. The stares make being out in public really unenjoyable.

You decide to bring the baby to KAF again. Why? You do not know. Maybe you enjoy the attention, or maybe it is just the iced ciders and croissants. That's beside the point. While waiting in line, the baby smiles at everyone around and attracts quite a bit of attention. You finally make it to the front of line, a line that was all the way out the door, and you begin ordering. You find out the card machine is broken, and the only payment accepted is declining balance amount (DBA), the school's Monopoly money.

The sweet student that was playing with the baby is an absolute saint and uses her DBA to cover your cider and yogurt. You quickly learn that not all students judge you for having a baby or make assumptions. They enjoy her cuteness and let you skip lines or treat you to coffee. Afterward, you make your way to the bathroom and get a bewildered look when a student exits and sees the baby. The difference in reactions becomes quite entertaining.

People begin to recognize you, and students from your class stop by when they see you to say hi to her. One of the students says you are "soooo brave" for being a "young mom on campus." He even mentions it in a frat and laughs when everyone's head turns toward you and the question downpour begins. All the questions seem to end with people being impressed and saying they would have been amazed if you did have a kid; they didn't think any negative comments were warranted. They thought anyone who was able to go to college while raising a family was admirable.

You begin to feel better about bringing her to campus—empowered even. That is, until a student mumbles, "just drop out already" as he passes you. Things like this never stop you from doing what you want; if anything, they push you harder to do them. You spend afternoons on the green with the baby teaching her to walk while holding your hands and playing airplane. People stop and smile, but you are so focused on the smiley baby in front of you that they do not matter.

People start asking you if you know other students with babies, and you actually do. You have this little friend group of students with babies. One is your best friend who you knew prior to your time on campus, but the other is one you constantly passed during walks around. He wears his baby son with a big coat over them to keep warm. You're babywearing, too. When you see each other, you give a little head nod that says, "I get it."

One of the other things you find yourself doing is noticing all of the changing tables on campus. There is one in the Hopkins Center and one in a bathroom in the library. You spot another makeshift table in the other library. It is more of a countertop, but it works.

None of the dining spaces have highchairs, so the baby is always sitting on your lap. One of the skills you've taught her is how to drink out of a normal cup with the help of an adult. Everyone in the dining hall finds this very impressive, and her high-five skills. You get a little confidence boost thinking you're teaching college kids some parenting/childcare tricks.

Anytime you park on campus with the baby, you laugh slightly. You're pulling up in a Tesla with falcon-wing doors. You park, watch the students stare a little, and then watch the stares intensify when you get the baby out. All you can think is that they are wondering one of two things: "Who is she married to?" or "Who is her sugar daddy?" Your close friends talk about pick-up lines you can use when frat guys notice the baby. It becomes a little inside joke with you and them. You hang out on campus, research people's reactions to babies, and start to understand more and more this stigma we have created around young parents.

The boys in your class who have never given you a second glance smile when they see you with the baby. You end up striking a conversation with one that leads to an unexpected friendship—a perk of the baby coming along? One day in class, you are leading your small group's discussion and end up bringing the baby. You meet everyone in the library and enter a glass-walled study room. Everyone can see that you have a baby with you. You hold her while you lead the group, and when she starts to get fussy, you go to take a seat. The chair slips from underneath you, and you fall into a squat position, catching your fall. You close your eyes and hope nobody notices, but when you open your eyes, the professor is staring, and a student is trying to give you his chair. You pull yourself together, sit in your seat, and continue the group discussion. You eventually get the baby to sleep, and the group wraps up. A friend invites you to lunch downstairs, and you bring the baby along. You two pretend that you're the baby's parents, and every-one says she has your eyes. They admire her cuteness, and you thank them. You laugh about it the whole way home.

During that class in the glass study room, there was a student staring at you before you entered the room. He kept looking at the baby. You connect on Instagram, and it takes you a while to recognize him from that baby-staring contest. He is very cute. Not the puppy-dog cute, but the pierced-ear and tanned-skin type. You used a pick-up line that you weren't proud of, but it was a complete joke: "She's not my baby, but you can still call me mommy." Weird thing is, it worked! He flirted right back.

One of the best parts about bringing her along is the way it makes the faces of staff light up. The boy in KAF who makes faces and smiles at her, the professor who waves hello from across the hall, and those who stop to say how nice it is to see a baby on campus because that doesn't happen often. You begin to understand why parents need to take their babies out often. The attention and adult interaction is needed when you spend all day at home talking to yourself and a four-month-old. You get a little stir crazy.

The mom you work for tells you to embrace it and just pretend she's yours. The reactions do make you laugh, but then she comes up with a wonderful response, "I own my business, paid for my car in cash, have a house, and this isn't even my baby." You use the line, adding, "But keep staring if you want to."

You might stop taking her to campus when your nanny gig ends, but on weekends, you'll start bringing the twins you work with. Those stares are even better. That one day you took them on a run in the double stroller while wearing a sports bra. Those stares you got were quite entertaining. The way people looked at you, like, "Wow! She bounced back after twins!"

It gets a little bit funny when you start dating people on campus and they tell you they recognize you from the library. You wonder how they forgot you had the baby with you while you were in the library. Apparently not everyone noticed her.

You'll find it interesting how many people just assume she is your daughter. If you were in any other college town, it would not have been shocking to be a nanny, but at this particular Ivy League school, the only rational explanation anyone can come up with is that she is yours and that you are being supported by rich parents. Nobody can imagine that it is just a job, maybe because of the heavy study workload, or maybe because the majority of students come from higher income households.

Either way, you take pride in knowing you are exposing students to a more diverse student body and waking them up to the real world. You even end up making an Instagram account called "dartbabies," highlighting all of the students with babies and what their lives looks like on campus.

During the pandemic, you take a break from baby-campus adventures for safety reasons and because nothing is going on, anyways. When you do return, it feels bizarre being stared at again. You grab some food from the campus food truck and share it with the baby on the green, enjoying a wholesome picnic and teaching the baby new skills like drinking from a water bottle.

As you walk around campus, you notice people looking you dead in the eye and just glaring. You're wearing a mask, so the glare isn't pandemic-related. You assume it's because of the baby and sink back into the awful feeling of heartbreak for the young parents on campus dealing with this daily.

You start to walk down frat row, baby strapped to your hip thanks to the ring sling. As you walk around, you get an idea, another way to shock students and make them realize just how judgmental they are.

Any time you bring the baby to campus, you do this thing where you walk toward a frat house and say, "Okay, sweetie, are you ready to meet your daddy? I think this is the frat he's in. Or maybe it was that one? Hmm. I guess I was really drunk the night you were conceived," laugh, and then make direct eye contact with whoever is staring. If you're going to do a social experiment involving babies on campus, at least have some fun and enjoy it, right?

The more often you bring the baby around the school, the less judgy the reactions are. People will begin recognizing her and waving from afar. That joke about being a brave, young mom gets even funnier, and you joke even more with your friends about your past and how this baby came to be. Everyone thinks it's funny to come up with different stories about how you got pregnant in college and how you were able to stay in school.

Your friend who has a baby and is married to a student uses friends on campus as babysitters. Sometimes, they even watch the baby in the dorm. You laugh with your friend about what it might be like if you actually did go back to school with a baby, playing pass the baby in order to avoid childcare expenses but still able to go to class. Each friend would just have to take the baby for thirty minutes until you were out of class.

The whole point is that even if this baby were yours and conceived during a drunken hookup at a frat party, that doesn't mean you can't be a wonderful mom or finish school. No parent should feel guilty about raising a baby while working toward their goal. We do not shame PhD students for having children or grown adults for having their kids go to the grandparents for childcare. Nobody is raising a child on their own, not even single parents. It takes a village, and we cannot shame college students for having a village that looks slightly different.

WHAT EXACTLY IS ONE SUPPOSED TO DO DURING WINTER IN NEW HAMPSHIRE?

～～

New England is an interesting place to live. The winters are brutal and leave you wanting to spend your days snuggled up in your dorm room. The sidewalks are slippery, and you don't enjoy your walks to class. You're in a grumpy mood because the cold weather feels like it is freezing your soul along with your body. The school plans some events to make the winter a little less boring, but the most fun you'll have is at events your friends plan. Winter carnival is one of those school-planned events. A polar bear plunge swim, human dog-sled race, dollar ski day at the slopes, and amazing ice sculptures made by students. Families from town join in on the fun, and it really is just a wholesome winter day.

Once nighttime hits, however, it gets a little more college-like. Students throw parties and drink a lot, all the ice sculptures start getting knocked down, and the out-of-state students learn how to really sled from the northerners.

Students use whatever they can as sleds. You see people sliding down icy hills on trash can lids and even riding bikes down. Surprisingly, nobody really gets injured; the amount of alcohol in their system is a decent anesthetic.

During the first snow, you'll head out for a snowball fight at midnight on the green. This isn't something you assume is happening, an email from Dr. Suess and Robert Frost is how students find out. The email will get forwarded to you by one of your friends, they always do. In fact, after this experience, you'll probably have a whole folder of emails from the president that students have screenshot and sent you. You stay in the loop.

If it is too cold outside, don't worry. You don't miss out on winter activities if you don't like the cold, you just move them to the dorm hallways. Students can be found using their skis on the staircases.

In the summer, there aren't as many students on campus. It's called "sophomore summer" because in order to navigate the housing shortage, the school needed to require one class to come for summer term each year, and the sophomores must've drawn the short stick.

The sophomores do know how to have fun, though. You can find the majority of them diving off Quechee Bridge and cliff-jumping at the copper mines; although, after some blasting was done at the mines, that was labeled an unsafe jumping location. Quechee Bridge seems to be the most popular spot. You'll notice huge groups of young adults dispersed at various jumping spots ranging in jump height.

The best summer activity is Green Key, but that takes place before spring term ends, sort of like a summer send off before the majority of students go home. One of the best traditions you'll hear about from alumni is the "float the river day." Students create insane floats with slides, lawn chairs, tiki torches, and minibars. They create the most elaborate float they can, and everyone spends the day floating on the river on their little creation while drinking. Somehow you'll all make it back to campus safely, despite the intense amount of alcohol consumed.

Drinking in local bars is tough in the summer because with all the alumni back in town and other college students home for the summer break, the bars begin getting a little stricter on carding people—thank the town police for that. The location of the school is wonderful if you enjoy outdoor activities, but you'll find the nightlife to be quite nonexistent. Every time the college gets a new president, he or she has to get approved by the town police, and usually that is done by them making an effort to show they want to reduce underage drinking on campus. You learn about this when people explain why you'll get expelled for bringing hard liquor on campus. Banning liquor was the president's way of trying to lower alcoholism rates. Who can blame him for trying? Wasn't the creator of AA a Dartmouth student?

One of the biggest events as students return to campus in the fall is homecoming. A giant bonfire takes place on the green. You'll drive past the wood tower in complete confusion wondering what was going to be taking place there. You'll later discover it's the homecoming fire. Freshmen run laps around the fire, sweating and laughing—twenty laps if you are graduating in 2020. The fire is roughly thirty-five feet tall. It is an event you will remember for sure.

When you get bored of these activities or they are canceled due to a pandemic, you'll start asking around for ideas on what else to do. Frating is everyone's first suggestion, but a pandemic means none of that . . . unless you know who's throwing the secret parties, that is.

In the summer you could kayak or hit up the pond if you're looking for something more wholesome than the Ledyard Challenge, a challenge that involves streaking on the Ledyard Bridge at the Dartmouth Outing Club (DOC). It's a good time for hiking because you're right near the Appalachian Trail and don't have to worry about the special gear that is necessary during winter hikes.

You probably won't find anything to do in the midst of the pandemic. Most likely you'll just get a lecture about how "you Dartmouth students will never appreciate what you have in front of you." You love nature but just want to spice things up a bit. Townsfolk love to tell off Dartmouth students and make them all appear like stuck up, snobby trust-fund kids.

WHY DO YOU WANT TO FIT IN ON CAMPUS SO BADLY?

〜

You find yourself having this huge desire to be accepted by everyone. Is it because you know you're different? Do you feel you don't belong because you aren't there for the same reasons as everyone else? It's like high school again—that feeling that you should conform to what everyone wants you to be. The difference here is that you have more experience, letting a certain side of your personality shine in order to impress the people you're with. You've done it in job interviews, while networking, and during class. You've mastered this to the point that it is an art. Nobody can see through it because it's not a lie. You aren't pretending to be something you're not; you're simply letting the parts of you these people will like show more than the other parts. This isn't the part of yourself you enjoy showing the most, though. You would much rather show off your "spunky hippie-dippie, lover-of-Earth" self, not that "stuck-up WASP family spending weekends at your cabin" side.

You're a relatively humble person but obviously proud of your accomplishments. You care about others and like to converse with new people. You make an effort to broaden your perspective in order to continue to learn more and do better. You quickly discovered the frat boy stereotype and saw the way they had a certain level of entitlement in how they acted on campus, but you weren't expecting this everywhere you went.

In class one day, you mention to your small group that you're tired when class ends early. You say it in a way that makes you appear grateful class ended a little early. A student lets out a little laugh and starts listing the reasons she is more tired than you. It doesn't matter that you run your household, care for your animals, take classes, and work eighty-hour weeks during this time in your life. You are not allowed to think even for a second that you are as tired as students. You get it—the workload is a lot—but this appearance of doing the most and being the most at everything is a bit much. You get the students who talk about being tired so as to appear to be busier and more successful. People who mention they are not getting enough sleep suggest they have a lot going on and are, therefore, more successful. You make a mental note to just keep your complaints to yourself.

You find out that there is a certain mold these college students were forced into, and it not only disgusts you but also worries you. You could not find one student who was not trying to do a million things at once. It was eye-opening to be surrounded by so many other overachievers, but it was cause for concern. Where did this idea come from? Why do we put students under so much additional stress? How are these the "good ol' days" if they are filled with so much anxiety?

The frat party scene is another place you find yourself trying to fit in. At a friend's house, a student shows you how to open a drink without a bottle opener. He takes you to the kitchen, reminds you not to do this trick on certain countertops, and gets ready to demonstrate. Due to the kitchen countertops being cheap, he shows you on the fridge door. You place the cap of the bottle so that it is resting on the door edge, hold the door still, and then slam your fist down on it. This little trick makes you instantly well respected at parties. It's one of those "I know what I'm doing" moves.

It isn't just about feeling smart and showing off at parties. You're actually trying to make friends and possibly even date someone. You know that dogs are a great conversation starter, so you start bringing your pup to the green. This seems like a great idea. He'll run up to a cute boy, and you'll gracefully chase after him, strike up a conversation, and the rest is history. The only issue is that your dog loves to pull you around, so trips to the green tend to end with you getting pulled to the ground. He's a mark-his-territory kind of pup, but not the way most are. He poops. Everywhere. Nothing attractive about bending over to scoop poop every five minutes. However, you quickly learn another way to use your dog to get dates. The football frat has a dog Instagram account, and you can slide into their DMs to set up a puppy playdate that will hopefully turn into a real date for you.

You notice another dividing factor between you and students is that you have a car. A lot of students are from the West Coast and were unable to bring their car with them. It makes you a little more well liked, but constantly paying for campus parking is something you find extremely annoying.

It's no secret to you by this point that other students like to analyze you. Someone will even point out that the lack of pastels in your wardrobe proves you aren't a real Hanover resident. One of those things they like to analyze is your vocabulary. Even if you are the most intelligent person in the class, you still make sure to incorporate just enough slang terms to remind everyone you're a student. You'll hear someone go into depth about the opioid crisis and drug issues in America but finish the sentence off by saying the situation was "sus," meaning suspicious. The professor doesn't seem to bat an eye at this type of verbiage, but it makes you cringe a little every time. You get called out for using your own choice of slang words like "deadass." People want to know why you're saying that if you aren't from the city.

If you get confused by a term, check Urban Dictionary before asking the person to explain. You don't want to look out of place, and most definitions are on UD. You hear new words like "simp" when you enter the dating world and a guy holds a door open for you or listens to your long rant when he just wants to get laid. You're made fun of for not shortening professor to "prof" and King Arthur Flour to "KAF." "FaceTimey" is used to describe people who hang in high-traffic areas in order to get noticed (you'll probably do this at some point). You'll pick up on nicknames, like "blobby" to describe Baker Library. Cuffing season is when everyone gets together to avoid the loneliness and cold of winter. A new term will start popping up, but that one is all thanks to you. You come up with "spring cleaning" to describe the breakups that happen right after cuffing season ends.

You'll notice the Greek letters spelling "THOT" on the front of one house, a closed-down sorority that, weirdly, is an acronym meaning "that ho over there."

The seemingly odd analysis you find yourself under often is not uncommon on campus. You'll discover lots of students who don't fit into that classic mold. Your first Dartmouth boyfriend will be vocal about how hard it was for him to go to a school where the children of WASPs overshadowed everyone else. You'll see the entitlement dripping from them anytime you try to talk about a success you had. Pride is good when you aren't putting others down, but they don't see it that way. Someone will ask you about the fancy new car you bought, you know, the Tesla Model X with falcon-wing doors. They'll see you driving it to class, but they'll assume it was just bought with daddy's money, a sweet sixteen or graduation gift.

How do you expect that car to be even slightly impressive when everyone is driving Range Rovers and your classmate's dad is the CEO of the Hasbro toy company? When talking to students, you find it easier to bond over your dad being a professional triathlete and him driving a Porsche than talking about relatable passions and research work you are doing.

Inclusivity on campus is important to the administration. They are making bigger efforts to use gender-inclusive terminology despite professors still greeting their class with, "Good morning, ladies and gentlemen." You can spot a few gender-neutral bathrooms on campus, though it'll never seem like there are enough. Those co-ed frats seem to provide welcoming spaces, especially when they stop using the term "brothers" for frat members and switch to "siblings." But even after Dartmouth allowed women into the school, the inclusivity was never fully felt there. Maybe it's because they were the last Ivy to let women in? Maybe it's because there are legends about sexist beer pong?

There is just something there making you feel that if you aren't a sorority girl from a small, nuclear, WASP family with a car you got as a graduation gift and a scholarship from years of playing volleyball, then you just don't fully fit in there.

Eat there, even if you don't go there. Finding out the best spots to eat on campus is a great way to meet cool people and fit in. Recommending things like the cookie party made you well liked, but knowing the best spots to eat gets you in with the cool people and makes doing work on campus more enjoyable. Those turkey and gouda sandwiches in Novack are addictive, but make sure you grab one before the football players snag everything from the pastry window. You'll find acai bowls in Collis that will make you wonder if Dartmouth has a little culture or is just being trendy.

It's hard to find that feeling of fitting in when there are secret societies all over town and campus. Like the one right next to Murphy's, which eventually just becomes a co-ed house because too many people know about it and break in. Another fun activity: breaking into secret societies.

Going back to this idea of stereotypical students, you were always the type of person that had a fire in their belly and was full of passion. You know who you are. Maybe you value others' opinions and like to hear them, but you choose what you know is right for you. The whole point of not going to college is choosing the path that is truly right for you, correct? So how did you end up conforming to the God-awful standards these students set for you? Why did you feel it was so necessary to try to fit in? Why mention your dad's victory in the Sweden UltraTri to appear like you came from a nice household like so many others? Talking about your dad's Porsche, the sauna in your living room, the weekends spent at your cabin in Boone . . . you went on a spiral of sinking to their level, further and further down, losing sight of your values. You value kindness, empathy, understanding, passion, ambition, and the ability people have to make you feel light. All of a sudden you cared more about who could get you into parties, set you up with the cutest fraternity members, or get you into the best events on campus. How could this level of conformity, conformity into such a negative mold, be okay? Everyone who achieves greatness is just a little bit odd, and those odd members of our communities are so important to the growth of humanity, yet we send people off to institutions where somehow they end up changing who they are and how they act. They become a little less odd and a little more like everybody else.

One day in class, your friend isn't there. It's one of the first few days of class, so you don't know anyone yet. You look around but can't find a seat except for one in the back with the football players. Screw it, you're sitting back there. You try to find ways to fit in. Laughing at a joke in hopes that they'll notice you and start a conversation, but they don't. You sit there completely ignored and nonexistent to them. You might as well not have been there at all. Once again, you feel like you're in the high school cafeteria and have chosen the wrong place to sit. You sit with the jocks when you aren't one. They won't tell you to leave, but they will completely ignore your presence. Check your ego at the door because there is nothing like a bunch of stuck-up twenty-year-olds to remind you that you aren't as special as you thought you were.

You know what really makes you feel like an outcast? Trauma. The boy you fell for, the one who made you feel on fire, will end up moving hundreds of miles away. Shortly after this move, you'll find out you're pregnant. You'll be alone in your new house in Vermont with nobody but your dog. The boy you think you're in love with won't speak to you. Your best friend will be busy with her own life and blow you off, not even realizing what is happening in your life. How are you supposed to return to your college experience when you're pregnant and the baby daddy is a recent graduate on the opposite side of the country?

You finally tell him, and although he doesn't know what he wants to do, he is supportive of whatever you want. You feel like you're ruining his life. No college student who is a few weeks from graduating is ready for a baby; nobody ever really is 100 percent ready for one. You spend the day you told him in complete panic. Even though he doesn't know if he wants to be a part of the baby's life, he texts throughout that day to make sure you're all right. You have an appointment to check your HCG levels that day, and you end up finding out that the pregnancy isn't viable. You tell him immediately. He calls, he cries with you, and he tells you that he wants to support you through this. He checks in occasionally, but eventually life catches up, and he's gone again. He is able to return to his life like everything is completely okay and this never happened. He becomes a distant memory, the boy you first felt a moment of love with, but the memory of having another miscarriage before the age of twenty forever burns in the back of your mind. How are you supposed to go back to college life when you experienced another huge trauma? There aren't other students on campus talking openly about similar traumas. What's the solution? Breaking stereotypes and making yourself known for all the obstacles you made it through? Or adding resources and support groups to campuses so that you have safe spaces to discuss these things?

Being new to the college scene means you'll see some things you aren't sure are normal, like the punch in the frat trash can, but you learn to just go with it. One of the things you'll hear about is the way students support each other in their presentations. Not just students being kind to other students, but people in a specific friend group showing up for each other in order to make the person presenting look good. You'll hear about a student whose posse of sorority girls dressed in the classic *Clueless* outfit show up to cheer her on. She finishes her speech and they clap loudly before exiting the room; only there to listen to her and leave. This seems bizarre to you, but you figure maybe it's normal. This isn't the first time you've seen students invite peers to their presentations for some big research project they did, but not a random linguistics class.

The lack of diversity in town is evident to everyone, but maybe a little less so to Dartmouth students because they, at least, have diverse groups of students around them, or so you thought. A student begins talking to the baby one day, and he's talking in that funny baby-talk voice about random things. Then as the baby starts to laugh more and more, he says, "You're laughing because you like me, 'cause I'm brown." Even this student knew there weren't many people of color in the area. One thing you find yourself thinking about again is how lucky you are to have traveled the world and been exposed to other cultures and ways of life, something lacking in small-town New England.

DATING GETS WEIRD

~

D ating someone in college is strange. You're an adult, so things are a bit more serious, but you're still in school with graduating as your top priority.

It's even trickier to navigate when you're not actually a student. You're running a business, taking classes, and no matter how busy you are, your stresses will never compare to those your partner is facing. If you decide to date an Ivy Leaguer, just be prepared to constantly feel overshadowed or a tiny bit lazy by comparison.

There is a huge hook-up culture on Dartmouth campus—just research their STD rates. You'll notice it right off the bat when you get unsolicited dick pics from a defensive back football player. Thank you, number thirty-five! You'll watch him continuously remake his Tinder profile day after day. Matching with a girl, sexting her without consent, and then making another profile. He'll only put one picture on his page, one of him playing football. The combination of just one photo and the photo being sports-related is a pretty sure-fire way to know ahead of time he is looking for a one-night stand. A stress relief from the workload Dartmouth has dumped on him. You feel slightly bad for number thirty-five until you get that unsolicited picture of his penis.

Your first date with a student was your birthday. He attempted to give you a tour of campus, but you already knew where everything was. You were slightly impressed when he took you up to the observatory until you realized what that meant. You're sitting in the car together talking and he begins looking at your tattoos, getting closer every time he asks about one. Closer and closer until he is shoving his tongue down your throat. You try to just go with it: it's your birthday and you deserve to enjoy it, but every move he makes you feel yourself getting more uncomfortable and dry as the Sahara desert. You feel distracted, noticing people walking past the car. They can't see you, but you can see them. The position you're in is awkward and not enjoyable. Elon Musk did not design his cars for backseat hook-ups. You finally end things and apologize profusely. In all honesty, all you're thinking about is this boy you met months before in Athens. He tells you those apologies are unnecessary and to never ever apologize for telling someone to stop when you aren't into it. He says he'll stay in touch and even follows your business on Instagram, but you never hear from him after that. You learn that the observatory line is just like when a guy says, "I have something to show you upstairs. It's in my bed under my sheets." It's a stereotypical hookup spot on campus—not one of the Dartmouth Seven, but an easy one-night stand "spice things up" kinda place. You call your friend and your mom that night to talk to them about what happened. All you're thinking is that you need to call London boy.

You have some time off school coming up and already had the trip booked anyway. It's supposed to be a short trip to London, where you just stay with the boy you kissed in the streets of Athens. It isn't supposed to be a Nicholas Sparks moment or anything. Just a trip back to one of your favorite places in the world to see the people you met in Greece. You'll be visiting that boy you kissed, a friend you two met in the Athens hostel, and grabbing lunch with the family you stayed with a few years prior when you first visited London. You're over-the-moon excited. You're getting a break from college life and going back to your usual, wanderlusting self.

During the plane ride over, it'll be pretty empty. Most people have a row to themselves, and you consider moving to an empty row but decide to stay with the guy you're seated next to. The middle seat is empty, so you'll have some space. You start watching a movie. Randomly, the guy asks if you want his dinner—airplane food he isn't super interested in. You end the movie and end up laughing with him over the joys of travel. Before you know it, you're telling this random guy your entire life story. Turns out this happens to him often. The entire plane is full of sleeping people, but you two are talking and talking and talking, for seven hours. He gives you life advice and you give him some, too. You find out he is eleven years older than you, but you keep in touch. Occasional text messages talking about your electric cars, travel plans, and romances.

When you arrive at the airport, you are extremely nervous. You're so ready to shower and get settled in with your friends. The boy meets you at the airport, you hug, and begin the train journey to his flat. Soon, you're showered, unpacked, and cuddling with him. You meet his friends, cook together, watch movies, and spend a lot of time in bed together. The last thing on your mind is everything that happened at Dartmouth. You spend your nights drinking wine and kissing, your days seeing friends and exploring. You feel at peace. Your first day out exploring, the two of you go to the London Eye, standing together enjoying the views and each other's presence. He's the guy that holds doors for you and always holds your hand when you're walking around—something nobody had ever done before. You had kissed boys and hugged, but you had never been with a guy that just held your hand. This guy kissed you goodbye at 7 a.m. at the Athens train station and watched you until the train was completely out of sight. He was the boy that stood behind you on the escalators in the station always with a hand on your shoulder. He'd either sneak a kiss on the cheek or just hug you from behind, eyeing every guy that looked your way because you were his.

He wakes you up one morning with a kiss and heads to work. It's a flash of everything you thought you wanted in the future: a partner who kisses you good morning, makes you breakfast, goes to work, meets you for lunch, and checks in throughout the entire day. He makes sure you are getting from place to place safely and enjoying your time. You do some work online while he is at the gym. He comes back on a phone call and pulls the phone away from himself for a second to kiss you. He says, "Hi, honey," and you feel yourself melt. Life feels good. You two explore Tate Modern and kiss at the top when your friend isn't looking. You feel like all that happened at Dartmouth didn't really matter because, at this point, your college experience was just a few weeks of frat parties and attending class, not having made any friends yet. You haven't learned those big lessons that are going to come. You feel yourself falling harder. He cooks dinner, and while the food is in the oven he runs (literally) down the street to buy you a bottle of wine. You eat an amazing meal but make the bad decision of drinking way too much wine. You two head to bed because the truth is you're about to black out and can't really walk. Definitely not your finest moment. You finally tell him the way you're feeling—nothing like some liquid courage to get you to confess everything. You aren't in love, but you want to pursue something with him because, screw it, who cares if someone is in another country? If you like someone, you give it a try. He doesn't feel the same, not because he doesn't like you, but because he is nine years older and doesn't look at life with a sense of wonder anymore. He tells you that if he was nineteen, he would pack up and run away to America with you, but he just doesn't think life works that way at twenty-eight. It hurts your heart. How could someone lose that sense of wonder that is such an important part of who you are?

The airport goodbye is extremely romantic. It's that Nicholas Sparks moment again, but once you're back in America, it's all over. At first, you'll be hurt, but then you start to think about it a bit more. The two of you had joked that one day he'd find his Wonder Woman; that was your way of saying he would meet someone who would bring his sense of wonder back. How sad is that when you break it down? Spending your life waiting around for someone to make you excited to be alive, someone who will make you want to see the world, feel love, and light your soul on fire. You need to remember that you light your own soul on fire and never need some "wonder person" to come in and do that for you. You can't rely on anyone except yourself. That doesn't mean don't have people around or don't lean on others for support. Just remember that you truly have everything you need within yourself. You are nineteen, and you can feel free. You can spontaneously run off to London or kiss a boy or girl in a frat basement or fall in love with a person or with your life or with yourself. Honestly, you should feel that way at forty, but it's a bit easier at nineteen. Go have that soul-on-fire, free-as-a-bird life. You'll return to college readier than ever to embrace the experiences you could potentially have there.

It's a small college, and not too long after all of that, you find yourself dating someone new who happens to know the observatory dude. He is nothing like the observatory guy. Maybe it's because the boy in London taught you how someone should treat you and opened your eyes to the type of love you deserve, but you find yourself falling harder and faster than ever. He asks for consent, talks through things, and seems to genuinely care.

You're slightly awed by his intelligence, spirituality, and genuineness. The connection you feel is extremely strong and it scares you a bit. Things feel so serious, and that causes every moment to feel extremely intimidating, until you two kiss. Who would have thought that during this time on campus you would experience the first love-filled connection of your life? At this point in life, you realize all you had already experienced was lust, but this was so different. This was complete acceptance, undeniable attraction, and the most insane chemistry you could ever imagine. You made an Ivy Leaguer forget words. Every time you two kissed, he couldn't speak and all you could do was smile the kind of smile that was completely real, as if nothing else mattered, a "butterflies in your tummy" smile. It became a joke between you two, "Dartmouth boy doesn't do words." It could break you out of those serious intense moments and make you fall into each other's arms and lie together again. You spent a lot of time lying together in that weird apartment under the Asian-Italian fusion noodle place. It was a time full of laughs and self-discovery. You figured out a little bit more of who you were and what you wanted out of life, and out of yourself.

This experience will be the one you are most grateful for during your campus adventures. It's the moment you learned what love felt like. The way he held you and synced your breathing with his when you had a panic attack after falling and spraining your ankle. The way he was vulnerable and would share his deepest emotions with you. The way he encouraged you to do and be better, to read more, and to bake more because he knew you loved it and he loved trying the things you made. The time together was short, but it taught you that sort of love was possible for you, and it made you more confident in your life decisions going forward.

You learn that the feeling of being fully "moved on" is when you are able to reach out to that person and not care if they respond. You are able to look back on all that happened in that short period of time and be grateful for the lessons you learned, experiences you had, and being able to say you felt love and know what you deserve now. It wasn't perfect. He was busy and left you wondering a lot. It didn't work out because of the world pandemic, the lack of understanding with what the other person needed, and other factors, but you know that there was love there. That is an experience nobody can ever take from you.

During the few weeks you were pregnant but didn't know it and after things had ended with spiritual Dartmouth dude, you started trying to meet other people. You end up dating a Tuck student who's twelve years older than you. It's pretty great, actually, and you're really enjoying your time with him. Once you begin to realize you might be pregnant, you decide to end things before they get too serious. You have him over for dinner one night. You had to go to the store at 8 a.m. before work to grab salmon because it had sold out everywhere the days prior. After work, you cook an amazing meal. You don't have much of an appetite, though. The two of you move to the couch, and he begins breaking things off with you. You're visibly uncomfortable but end up relaxing and telling him you agreed with the decision. He's concerned with how it'll look if people discover he's dating someone so much younger for a short period of time before moving away. He says he isn't going to make any more moves on you but won't stop you if you make one. So, you do, and before you know it, you're on top of him and making out with him on the couch. He makes plans to come back to see you once more before he moves and texts you for a bit in the later weeks, saying he is there if you ever need advice or something. But then he disappears, and you never hear from him or of him again.

Oh, and he never knew you were pregnant. That didn't really seem relevant to mention when he was dumping you.

It's hard to return to the normal dating world after all of this, back to dating apps and the Netflix-and-chill thing. For example: the dreaded Tinder conversations and questions like, "What exactly are you looking for on Tinder?" One of the students you went on a date with really brought you back down to earth after your few, short weeks on cloud nine. He was a self-proclaimed degenerate rugby player. You're in his dorm chatting and then making out, but nothing more because freshmen in college are grossed out by periods and going further wasn't an option for him. He says he has to get back to studying. He walks you out to your car, which is parked behind the dorm building because he had told you to park there. It's around 1 a.m., and he happily says, "Your car is still here," as if it is a complete surprise. You look bewildered, and he explains that it is illegal to park back here without a staff parking pass. He had expected your car to get towed or booted. Once again you are reminded that most college boys care more about getting laid than they do about your safety when inviting you over in the middle of the night.

On one date, a guy will question something you talk about and says he'll look it up. You'll notice in his phone's reflection on his glasses that he isn't looking anything up but actually texting another girl.

Not being an actual student can make finding out about events and connecting with new people hard. How can you fix that? Social media. Just make an account that mentions Dartmouth in the bio and upload a cute profile pic. Set it to "private" and don't post anything in your stories unless it's a thirst trap. Then look up the roster for every sport you like and follow the ones you think are cute. This is how you'll find your campus crush and be able to swoon over him. You might even strike up a conversation with him by sliding into his DMs, and before you know it, you have a new friend on campus. You broke your anti social-media pact you made with yourself, but cute frat boys are worth it, right?

Throughout COVID times, you see new faces joining the Tinder world. Surprisingly, a lot of Dartmouth students. Many decided to come back to campus and decided to check out the Tinder world, mainly out of boredom. Things went from "Netflix and chill" to "quarantine and chill" real quick.

During COVID-19, you find yourself hanging more often with a friend from campus. You two take things a tiny bit further one night, and he ends up with a hickey on his neck. You think hickeys are fun. No, this isn't high school, but you think of it as a fun, little mark from a fun night that only the two of you know is there. The only issue is sometimes they're in places that everyone can see. Somehow, every hickey you give seems to last an extremely long amount of time and leaves a huge mark. The hickey you gave your friend covered the majority of one side of his neck and was really hard to cover. He was in an interview on campus and had to put a Band-Aid over it—very noticeable. You tell him to just own it, but he has fun making up stories as to why his neck is bandaged: bear attacks, dogs, angry EMT patients. All of the students that have hickeys during quarantine couldn't turn their heads during Zoom calls out of fear that people would notice. Has anyone ever figured out how to get rid of or cover a hickey?

Toward the end of this pseudo-college experiment, you begin doing some work with Dartmouth, wanting to focus more on research with doula work. You start setting boundaries to not socialize as much with students in advance. What do you do when a student starts flirting with you on Tinder? Of course, there are policies in place for dating people on campus and the whole "abuse of power" thing, but you can't help but laugh and encourage the conversation with this particular student. He sends a message saying, "No cap I lowkey saw you in lib and resulted to flitzing you." You have to break that down for people. "No cap" means he is serious. "Flitzing" is the flirty version of "blitzing," which is Dartmouth's term for email. You're a little confused because you usually have a baby with you on campus. He seems oddly supportive of the baby thing and wants to know how old they are and if they are yours. You joke that he can't flitz you now that you might be becoming a staff member, tell him the baby isn't yours, impress him with info on the business you run, and move on, laughing each time you think back to it.

If you decide not to date anyone on campus, you can still enjoy admiring the good-looking bachelors. The Green is a common place you'll see this happening. You see plenty of moms and babies on picnics while Dartmouth boys sunbathe shirtless. You can't help but wonder if the moms are sneaking a glance at the shirtless boys the same way you are. The only difference is you aren't so subtle with your glances. You want them to know you're looking so they'll come over and talk to you.

Despite all the failed attempts to catch a guy's attention, you still continue to try funny pick-up lines or weird tactics to strike up a conversation. You aren't the confident type. You know you're good looking, but you know there are others who are far better looking. Besides, everyone is attracted to different people, so looking pretty may not be enough to get a specific person to call you. You'll get most of your funny pick-up line ideas from accounts like "College Dropout," watching girls get guys by simply grabbing their hand and asking, "Where are we going?"

You're at a tire shop one morning, right at opening because your tires exploded on the side of the highway at 6 a.m. on your drive home from an overnight shift. Thank goodness for AAA and a friend willing to drive over and give you her car for the two weeks yours is in the shop. These are the moments you regret buying a fancy car. You notice two students at the tire shop as well. One with a sporty look, decent looking, and the other with a weird skater-boy messy haircut who is more your type, but your friend convinces you to flirt with sporty frat boy instead. Nothing like your nine-months pregnant best friend being your wingman early in the morning to make you excited for the day. She tells you to slip him your business card—cute, flirty, and impressive. Keep in mind your friend got married at twenty and doesn't know how frat boys act, but you go with it. It's awkward, embarrassing, and you are 100 percent sure he threw the business card away, but his friend had this strange look the entire time that made you wish you gave him your number instead. You leave with your friend to go get some errands done but quickly return to the tire shop because you realize those guys probably need a ride back to campus. Nope, they didn't. Now you're even more embarrassed as you drive away feeling like a complete weirdo.

Dartmouth may have turned you a bit boy crazy because you end up going to the pond with a friend, and all you two seem to do is talk about the hot tennis players. You decide you'll start playing tennis together. Pull up in the Tesla, play some tennis in cute outfits, woo all the boys. You even go buy the skirt. But while at her house, when you two begin making plans, you realize she is married and nine months pregnant, so no frat boy is going to talk to you when you're with her. This whole in-between college and typical adult life is a bit hard to navigate. Half of your twenty-two-year-old friends are married with kids and the other half are blacking out in frat basements multiple times a week.

Nobody can blame you for trying, though. Usually, you are pretty good at impressing guys. Like that time when you parked to go to the Green and you had the back doors of your car open. You could hear two guys talking loudly about the car, so you made direct eye contact. They smiled and said they thought your car was cool. Your friends said you should have asked them if they wanted to drive it, so the next time someone mentioned your car, you did just that. It happens often, students commenting on the car. Usually, you have the baby, so you assume they're wondering who you married or if you have some weird sugar daddy, but when you're alone you know they're impressed by it. Your favorite was the sweet boy who smiled one of the most beautiful smiles you've ever seen and simply said "that's sick, so cool" and continued to smile.

You'll become friends with a former Dartmouth student when he rents a room in your best friend's house. You'll be blown away by the little feeling of lostness he experienced post Dartmouth. He didn't leave feeling like he had all the answers. He traveled, hiked, and applied to law school. So, you wondered, what were all these lost students really learning here?

If you didn't get the chance to have the hook-up of your dreams don't fret. There is something called "last chances." You submit the name of the person you like, and if they submitted your name too, you are able to get together. A great end-of-year final hook-up opportunity.

THE ONE THAT GOT AWAY . . . I'M GLAD HE DID

That boy who showed you what love felt like; the one that set your soul on fire, intimidated you, and encouraged you to do what you love all at the same time, will be referred to as the one that got away. That's what it felt like. He left campus after an incident with some students that made him realize he really didn't even want to fit in with the other Dartmouth students. He went to New Mexico with his best friend until he figured out his next steps.

You noticed your abandonment complex after this, constantly feeling left. He didn't leave *you*, though. He left a toxic environment that wasn't allowing him to grow. But it won't hurt any less.

He was the boy that made plans to do things that brought you great joy. He listened to your concerns and cried with you. You walked together at your favorite trail in town. He enjoyed all of the treats you baked. You danced around your living room at 3 a.m. to "1985" by Bowling For Soup in your pajamas. He watched your favorite Disney movie and ate Chinese food on your couch in your new house. This is the boy who admired your spiritual beliefs and made an effort to understand each part of you. He was the one who reached out after your Murphy's harassment situation.

When you look back on the relationship you two had, you will wonder why you are the type of person who gets so attached and if the connection was as strong as you thought. You'll blame your feelings on the effects of quarantine during a pandemic but will hold with you those skills he taught you like breathing in sync with someone during panic attacks. You'll remember how much of a powerhouse you are and stop caring so much about the opinion of frat boys.

You'll get all the animals you want and can handle because you want to, despite him thinking it's a weird idea to get chickens. Your decisions aren't made with him in mind anymore because he showed you that your opinion is the only one that really matters. They are your own. Again, you are free: completely and utterly yourself, grateful for the love you had for this boy because it reminded you that you don't want that kind of attachment and that you aren't the kind of person people stereotype you as. You're able to go forth and do better for yourself because of this odd quarantine romance. Nothing like being stuck home alone and completely deprived of human contact to make you fall head over heels for a frat boy. And, after all, if you love someone, set them free; if they don't come back, they weren't yours in the first place.

He wasn't the one that got away. He didn't leave you. He did what was best for him, and if people see that as selfish, well we should all be a little more selfish.

Please go be selfish. Remember this: you are allowed to be angry at him for not loving you the way you loved him. Just don't let it consume you. Were you really in love with him or were you in love with who you became when you were with him?

Learn the lesson that not every relationship is "The One;" sometimes they are the one that'll teach you something important, like how to be treated or how to love and be loved. It's okay to hold on for longer than others might, but feel how good it is to let go and be able to just *be*.

HIGH AS A KITE, BAKED LIKE A CAKE

~

The drug scene isn't massive on campus regardless of what the Internet and books about Dartmouth say. You credit that to the fact that it's the middle of nowhere and drugs are hard to come by unless you drive to another state where marijuana is legal or you join the opioid crisis in Manchester, NH.

It's a bit shocking, the lack of drugs, but in a good way. The only time you really hear about drugs on campus is when a bong catches fire in a fraternity garbage can and the fire trucks come, or when someone mentions that Bones Gate is known for hard drugs like the white snow and H.

Drugs seem to be common in other Ivy League schools because of the amount of stress students are under, but the majority of Dartmouth students who use them are forced to detox due to lack of a supply on campus.

You will witness a couple strange drug-related moments on campus at parties. Like the time that your date to a party abandoned you in his room to go get high with some friends. You have no idea what he took, but instead of kissing you goodbye, he fist-bumped you. Probably one of the most awkward goodbyes you've had after a frat party bedroom make-out session.

You hear a little bit on the Dartmouth Reddit page about how one student didn't think he would make it through college without a heavy drug intake, but other than him and that awkward goodbye, you don't see much in the way of drugs. Of course, you see the odd stoner here and there. On a date, a guy offers you a bowl and says he smoked just before . . . what is up with guys getting stoned before dates?

You notice socks on smoke detectors in frats and dorms so students can get away with smoking inside. For the most part, though, they simply open their windows. You might hear someone talking about edibles, but it turns out they were only talking about an edible arrangement of fruit they got from their aunt.

The milk and cookies party starts becoming known as a great pre-smoke spot once you tell everyone they can grab a bunch of cookies then leave. Perfect smoke snack. Girl Scout Cookie season is a blast and quite funny once you learn a stoner story from a friend. He offered someone a cookie, and they reached in the box to grab one, waved their hand around, and pulled it out empty. The person offered him one again and he said he could already taste them, just from waving his hand around.

Eventually you make friends with some people in town and hear a little more about the town's view on Dartmouth. Most see the students as reckless, who don't look before crossing the street and drink way too much. Most of the students get their drugs from the town dealer, an adult about ten years older than the students who frequented Dartmouth frat parties and deals to students.

BACK OUT OR BLACK OUT

~

The moment you decide how your night is going to go is based on the question, "Keep drinking or back out?" Getting "shmacked" on campus is everyone's favorite pastime. Dartmouth is a "work hard, party harder" type of school mixed with the saying, "go big, or go home." You're going to hear about a lot of interesting moments on campus.

It's amazing when you really take a moment to notice the creativity students have. They're able to turn all sorts of normal games into drinking activities. Drunk Monopoly, drunk cornhole, strip Twister—even Candy Land can be turned into a drinking game. The students really worship drinking. Their unofficial mascot is "Keggy the Keg." You can even find him on Tinder, an account run by some bored sophomore who admits he is desperate to get laid.

One of the first things you'll probably notice is the safety hazards. Living in the north, it's scary making your way back to your dorm in the cold. The ground is slippery, and you can't tell how cold you actually are because alcohol warms you up. You feel a little too invincible. A lot of students make it back to their dorms, but can they make it back inside? You'll hear of students getting locked out in the cold way too often. Luckily, campus security finds them.

Dartmouth students don't believe they drink more than other colleges, and frankly, during your time on campus, you probably won't witness too many crazy drunk moments, but the lack of nightlife in New Hampshire does make drinking occur more frequently. Compared to other colleges you've visited, the amount per night will probably be the same, but the amount of drinking nights per week is increased. You'll also wonder who chose what nights parties are thrown on because who wants to be drunk on a Tuesday or Wednesday night?

Dartmouth may lead the Ivy Leagues in drug and alcohol violations, but you'll notice how the school's location may be part of that. Maybe if there was a stronger nightlife and more going on in town, people would have better things to do than drink. Does the amount of stress students are under play a role too?

Most people think of partying when they hear "Dartmouth," even if they haven't been. The media has built it up as a huge party school, and that isn't hard to do when the only social world you have in town is Greek life. Dartmouth even sent out an email during your time on campus saying that you don't have to partake in Greek life and that you can just hang at your boyfriend's fraternity with his friends or in your dorm alone, as a way to remind students that if you want a social life you need to join Greek life.

In your health disparities class, you will discuss Dartmouth drinking rates, comparing the amount of people who don't drink before arriving to the amount of freshmen drinkers, and then seniors. It seems that almost every student engages in underage drinking during their time here. How would you even avoid it when one of the first things you learn is Dartmouth pong?

You find that the cold doesn't play such a big role in alcohol consumption as you thought. How could it with so many other schools with low drinking rates being in the north? Students drink because they want to. You wonder if it is a regional thing, with so many growing up on the West Coast in higher-income areas. These students weren't shy to the party scene, so were they just worsening habits they already had?

You found that Dartmouth alumni thought the amount students were drinking wasn't practical in the real world and learned that many students looked forward to the classic Dartmouth post-graduation detox.

Looking back, you begin to realize that you stopped drinking and sobered up for good after the pandemic hit. In the moment, you thought you were simply enjoying parties and a break from work, but college was turning you into an alcoholic. Now, looking back, you won't regret any of it because it opened your eyes to your addictive personality and unstable mental health in a more controlled setting. That sounds kind of bad. What I mean is that you'll realize that you were overworking yourself and handling it Dartmouth-style: lots and lots of alcohol. It's not to say that you are some crazy addictive person and can't ever do anything without getting attached. It was just an eye-opener to where you were at in life: a place where you were under way too much stress and handled it with what was right in front of you. It's a bit odd to you, though, the way you started drinking at Dartmouth after years of attending high school and college parties completely sober and disgusted by the idea of drinking. Was it because of your recent European travels and the drinking habits that developed there? Or was it because drinking at Dartmouth is inevitable, and you were tired of saying no and not fitting in despite everyone telling you it was okay not to drink? How can you feel so pressured to drink when everyone continuously says they are anti-peer pressure and constantly tell you it's okay to drink water? What kind of reverse psychology witchcraft is that? It probably has something to do with the fact that you didn't trust the people you were around in high school and didn't want to drink and do something stupid around them. Something about the drinking environment at Dartmouth felt more comfortable and trustworthy to you.

The first time you ever got invited to a fraternity, you were extremely nervous, so you drank a vodka cranberry before. It hit you harder than expected, way more vodka than cranberry, huh? You didn't feel comfortable driving, so you texted the guy you were supposed to meet. He lectured you on how stupid it was to drink and how he thought you were better than that. You asked him what he was planning to do with you at the frat. He said he planned to drink with you, so where did this weird lecture come from? His better-than-thou stuckupness was showing.

The amount of drinking definitely contributes to unfortunate events on campus. Safe Rides can help with that, allowing students to return to their dorms without getting stuck out in the cold, sleeping in a random frat, driving drunk, or possibly ending up in a situation they never wanted to be in.

Not all students make bad decisions while drunk or end up in places they don't want to be. You meet a group in Phi Tau that forms a "cuddle puddle" when drunk. They all cuddle on beanbags and laugh together. You even find them having a tickle fest one night. All is fun and games until someone is knocked on the ground and ends up with a concussion, though.

You'll spot some guys choosing a different type of activity outside on the Green: attempting to climb trees and hang upside down. Pretty fun to watch, but the best part is when they hide in the trees until someone walks past. Then they swing down, yell "boo," and scare everyone. Drunk people pranking and scaring each other is a great entertainment source.

There aren't a lot of students with tattoos, at least not as many tattoos as you. They become a topic of conversation quite often, and one night, you and a girl are chatting about them in the Phi Tau kitchen. You start talking about the massive thigh tat you got in Athens, and before you know it, your pants are off and you're showing her all your tats. You feel self-conscious because you aren't wearing cute underwear, but drunk girls always hype each other up. She's going on and on about how cute your thong is, and once again, you feel confident that you're hot and can score any boy you want. You're thankful for the confidence boost and the new party friend you made.

You will witness a bit more of this strange drinking environment in places like the hipster frat, where students drink the house's signature drink while wearing strange outfits in the afternoon.

What will you decide: get so drunk you pee your pants multiple times, or stay in for a Netflix-and-chill night? Just always remember to wear flats when drinking. No more falling down the stairs in Murphy's every time you go to the bathroom drunk. Maybe that's why you peed your pants . . . stairs are hard to navigate drunk.

Make sure you secure a place to crash. Dartmouth students may think texting and driving is wrong, but they'll encourage drunk driving home. You don't want to take the saying "place to crash," literally.

WHY WERE YOU SO SCARED OF FRATS?

~

The weirdness of drinking culture and the dating scene may be a bit much to process, but it won't be terrible for you because you'll have this strange feeling of safety thanks to Title IX.

As a survivor of multiple occasions of sexual assault, this is something very important to you, having a place to go to when you receive unsolicited dick pics or you experience sexual harassment by a professor. They aren't great at dealing with the latter, you'll discover, but at least they helped with those pictures from that weird football player, right? No, as inclusive as campus is becoming, the lack of proper investigation in sexual harassment reports will drive you mad. Especially in a time when Snapchat exists and Dartmouth outside investigators can't prove nudes were sent via Snap, so students are let off with less than a slap on the wrist.

When you live in the middle of nowhere, you get bored easily. That leads to drinking, which inevitably leads to bad behavior and mistakes being made. Dartmouth has increasing reports of rape, which may be due to more students feeling comfortable making reports, but could also be due to frat and drinking culture.

It's clear to you that not all fraternity members are rapists and not all men are bad, but the touchiness alone that they have when drunk shows what they are capable of doing. We're teaching girls how not to get raped instead of teaching young men that this behavior is completely not okay.

During your time at Dartmouth, you'll learn they aren't usually in the news for good things. The sexual harassment lawsuit against multiple professors is one of the first things you hear about. It's honestly part of the reason you tried to avoid the school in the first place. Why would you want to hang out at a school that is known for paying off rape victims in order to keep things hush-hush?

The increase in rape was accompanied by reports of fondling, dating violence, and statutory rape. This can be credited to the #metoo movement. At first, it makes you not want to hang around Dartmouth. One of the first things someone in town said to you when you moved there was, "Don't go to frat parties at Dartmouth. You *will* get raped."

You were terrified. You refused to ever go to a frat alone. It turns out those rape rates increased because Dartmouth did try to better its resources for survivors. Things may not be perfect, but you were a bit more at ease, and eventually you felt comfortable and safe enough to meet friends at parties, and walking in alone wasn't terrifying anymore.

It turns out that the town creeps are who you should actually be afraid of. One night, you'll be out drinking in Murphy's with some friends. Before you know it, you are completely shitfaced. This night will be one of the worst of your life. The night began with you eating ice cream given to you by a friend from Pine. After, everything starts to blur together. That friend that you are with ends up trying to make a move and doesn't take no for an answer. The last thing you remember from the night is him trying to kiss you and then a faint memory of peeing your pants multiple times in your driveway later that night. You don't know how you got home. You have angry messages from that guy about how you should have just kissed him back. You somehow managed to wash your clothes you remember peeing all over. The blurry memory of walking inside completely naked and going to sleep that way haunts your mind, but all you can really focus on is him touching you, trying to kiss you, not leaving you alone all night, and then falling down the stairs on your way to the bar bathroom before everything went black.

You start getting flashbacks of the night, chugging a bottle of prosecco in the Tuk Tuk Thai alleyway, and then drinking a glass of wine and two neat Jack Daniels in Murphy's. But you don't remember ordering anything or buying any drinks, so someone please tell me, what was in your ice cream?

Just remind yourself this:

You're safe now.

You didn't hurt anyone; he did.

You're allowed to be angry.

Your feelings are valid.

He took advantage of you.

He was twelve years older.

No always means no.

You're safe now.

Whether it's peer pressure or someone roofieing you, you're being taken advantage of. Learn to keep yourself safe and set boundaries with groups you don't want to be associated with.

Granted, there will be one scary student on campus, one you are convinced is stalking you. You see him one night at the Tesla charging station, but no Tesla. Then at Michael's and at Boloco. All in the same night. You see him in King Arthur Flour; he's glaring at the baby you're with. It's a bit odd. You see him a few more times all over campus that day. It's a small town, so multiple sightings in one day isn't that odd, is it?

You keep seeing him until eventually you find out he is now in the class you're auditing. So, you do the obvious thing and reach out to the prof. She isn't worried until you give her the list of all the locations you saw him. She says to have your guard up. Someone notifies you of Title IX, just in case. Eventually, you ask a student for the class list. You circle all the guys' names, cross off the ones you already know, and begin looking up the ones you don't on Facebook. You find him. Of course, his name is one of your favorite baby names. Cross that name off your list and hate it for a bit.

He volunteers with the Salvation Army, plays with his cousins, and bottle feeds a baby in his photos. Definitely doesn't seem like the stalker type. Maybe the Upper Valley really is that small?

One day, a random student sits behind you in class. One who isn't in the class. You overhear him mention that he had a free hour and decided to come listen to the lecture, but the professor had just been notified about your potential stalker, so she is eyeing this student. She finally asks him who he is, in front of the whole class. He explains, and she's okay with it. It probably didn't help that he was typing away on his computer because she hates note typists, but class is back to normal after that and things feel slightly calmer. Poor guy was a bit embarrassed having to introduce himself, though. If only he had been there for the awkward second day of class introductions—those introductions may have been equally embarrassing.

EVERYONE LIKES A BIT OF A CHALLENGE

You can't stress this point enough when at Dartmouth: there isn't a lot to do. This college will definitely bring out your crunchy side. Hiking, cliff jumping, and kayaking are the most common things to do, but students have come up with an array of challenges to spice up their time in New Hampshire. These challenges will lead to some of the most memorable moments you have on campus.

The first challenge you'll hear about is the Ledyard Bridge challenge. New Hampshire and Vermont have different laws regarding public nudity, and the bridge just so happens to go over the state lines. You strip at the Dartmouth Outing Club (DOC), where you can rent kayaking and hiking gear or plan cabin trips and other outings that "stimulate interest in the out-of-door winter sports." Then, you swim across the river and attempt to run across the bridge back to your clothes before getting caught by town police. There are no rules about what time of day this has to be done. You'll find that COVID-19 is the perfect time because nobody is out, and police officers are on the highways doing car counts.

Next, you'll hear about the Dartmouth Seven. This one you'll find the most laugh-worthy. It consists of having sex in seven very public locations on campus before graduation day: the library stacks, the fifty-yard line, Dartmouth Hall, Presidents Lawn, The Bema (the outdoor amphitheater in College Park), top of the Hop, and the Green. Most students aim for at least one, but many try to complete them all. There are campus group chats that notify students when the police have finished an hourly patrol past a location, when lights go off in front of Dartmouth Hall, and when a couple has finished at one location and it is available to the next. This challenge is so well known, you might encounter lines of couples at certain spots on popular nights.

Students have a variety of tips for each other. Girls wear skirts and no underwear, and they choose partners who know what they are doing and will be quick. One night, you almost consider doing it. It's during COVID-19, so there aren't people out. You more than likely won't get caught, and you want to be able to say you did one, even if it seems incredibly risky and stupid. You decide maybe you'll do the fifty-yard line, but the more you think about it, the more stupid it sounds, especially because you just fell down the stairs under Noodle Station and caused permanent damage to your ankle. How exactly were you planning to jump the fence with an injured ankle?

Most people you befriend on campus haven't completed the challenges; others are keeping their victories a secret. The Bema is the most common Dartmouth Seven challenge people you meet have completed. It's probably because it's the easiest, hidden in the woods away from campus security patrols. It's also the most romantic: a beautiful secluded wooded spot.

After a while, you start to come up with your own Dartmouth Seven list. You notice a few places you think should have been on the list. Why do it in front of Dartmouth Hall when you could nut in front of McNutt instead? Why isn't the top of Baker Library in the bell one of them? Hooking up in a secret society seems like another one that should be on the list. Or maybe even in a canoe at the Dartmouth Outing Club or in a golf cart on the course?

The last challenge is the most wholesome. There is a popular local breakfast spot called Lou's. Students stay up all night to make it there at 6 a.m. for breakfast. You could stay up studying or you may have been up drinking, but the goal is to get there right when they open. You have to make sure you order the right thing, though, or you may end up absolutely hating the place. The donuts are always a win.

There are a few non-official traditions, as well. Like Tubestock, where you build a wooden raft and float down the Connecticut River binge drinking. Unfortunately, this was canceled in 2006 after two decades' worth of annual Tubestock events, but you'll still hear about it from alumni. Dartmouth also holds a Pow-Wow. A two-day celebration with traditional Native American crafts, dancing, and music.

Dartmouth is known for multiple streaking challenges, not just the Ledyard Challenge. What is up with students stripping or deciding to do the dirty in public places? Such a scandalous school . . . or maybe not; I mean, Yale has naked parties and orgies. Many students graduate with a misdemeanor for public indecency, but they view it as a badge of honor.

Dartmouth's biggest tradition is Green Key, their own little music festival. Green Key weekend involves a lot of drinking, even more than the typical Dartmouth student consumes in a weekend. They have pretty good artist line-ups, like in 2012 when ASAP Rocky performed. Hard to imagine pretty boy Flacko stepping foot in Hanover, though. Your friends will describe Green Key as Tomorrowland and an amusement park rolled into one. An experience unlike any other you'll have on campus.

There are a couple other random "challenges" or traditions on campus. Students referred to Gile Mountain as a must-do hike before graduation, so of course you did it. Just a mile hike to a fire tower, where you can see all the trees that surround Dartmouth and the top of Baker Library. It's nothing like the big hike Dartmouth students do during the freshman outing trip with the DOC.

Another thing you'll have to do is visit King Arthur Flour, not the KAF in Baker Library, but the big one only a few miles from campus. It's a classic Vermont thing to do, but also a great way for students to escape campus for an afternoon. This bakery is full of delicious foods, and don't even get me started on the gift shop. So many great house-warming gifts. You'll visit with your friend from class and end up buying gifts for family and friends. Nothing like lunch with a friend and the baby at a beautiful Norwich bakery to make you feel a little less like college students. You feel like a classic New Englander with the amount of fun little trips you take to KAF. Croissants and iced ciders for days.

There is also the challenge of guys trying to get laid. It's interesting what they'll do and how far they'll try to push you without taking no for an answer. There was this one preppy Asian student that just would never stop trying to kiss you. When you were in fertility treatment, when you were dating someone else . . . no just wasn't enough for him. So you block him. Don't feel bad about it. People need to learn that getting someone to sleep with you isn't a challenge, it's as simple as yes or no.

I FOUND GOD ON FRAT ROW

D artmouth isn't lacking in community if you're Catholic. One of
the best things on campus is the amazing community dinners in
the Catholic student house, ironically located at the end of Frat
Row. There's something humorous about such a Godly building in the
location of so many blackouts.

Although you aren't Christian, you do find yourself at a handful
of community dinners. Despite that your pagan witch-self feels out of
place, you don't feel as judged as you expected. You end up meeting
people who are able to answer your biblical questions in ways you
never knew you needed. Growing up in the Bible Belt, you had a lot
of confusion surrounding your idea of what Christianity actually is.

You meet a student minister who is able to provide you with an im-
mense amount of support during a hard time in your life, and although
you don't call yourself Christian, she shows you love as if you were.

Apologia is the Christian thought journal, a magazine distributed
on campus covering different topics from abstinence to if Jesus was
real. This is where you had the majority of your questions relating to
religion answered. You never really understood Christianity, but one
of the leaders of *Apologia* explained it all to you and gifted you a Bible,

which you may or may not have ever opened, but you appreciate more than he would ever know. The puzzle pieces all fell into place during that conversation in a Starbucks and you really understood where Christians were coming from.

Apologia hosted a fun event called "Text for Toasties" where students texted a question about God and an *Apologia* member delivered them a grilled cheese or Nutella sandwich with an answer. You were able to help with one of the questions and explain to some members why some may be turned off from Christianity by the lack of premarital sex and the feeling of having done something wrong, and being told how to live your life: all things you had struggled with.

You never thought you'd fit in, be accepted by, or become friends with a group of such hard believers, but there you were having all your suspicions and concerns explained in a way that made you even more accepting of people that believed different things than you.

BACK TO REALITY

~

Things eventually begin to return to reality for you. Students are home for break, and you are left in your quintessential New England town. Cliff jumping isn't as fun solo, and the Green is covered in families again. You begin to realize that Dartmouth was a bit of a diversity hub for the area, and without students, staff, and researchers, the town lacks the little culture it had. There is an old man playing trumpet on the Green, angry alumni talking about COVID-19, families playing frisbee, and couples roller skating.

Life is still busy for you, and you try to focus on work, but you feel like a great part of your life is missing. Those seemingly meaningless conversations in fraternity basements and nights that made you second-guess ever drinking again were weirdly important parts of your week.

You made fun of those who referred to college as the "good ol' days," but you begin to understand it. It wasn't the drinking, stress, or education that they longed for, but those movie-like moments. When you are laughing in a fraternity basement high on life with people you barely know but somehow love, you feel like you're dreaming. You can experience these moments when out traveling solo, but the way college forces you into a group of people you might not typically like and allows you to feel that is an awakening experience for many.

During your travels, you'll possibly experience this if you stay in a hostel and are willing to strike up conversations with random people. You might be forced into knowing someone during your travels in a weird universe-controlled way, like a pillow flying across the room like someone used telepathy. Then before you know it, you're laughing about the pillow with a random new friend. Those weird universe-controlled moments feel more rare because we have a moment of choice, to either say "that was weird" and move on or laugh about it and become friends with a random stranger. Most anxious travelers won't choose the latter and will miss out on forming friendships that bring those dreamy movie-like moments into your life. College really forces you into social situations that push you out of your comfort zone in ways life can't if you aren't willing to take the leap.

At the end of this experience, I truly believe that college is not for everyone and that the vital experiences college provides one with can be found elsewhere, but you have to be willing to look for them. There are so many paths to get there, and we will all end up where we are supposed to be, even if it doesn't seem that way. Just know that your life is your own. You can go to a trade school and spend your weekends partying at a college frat, or you can travel the world and study remotely. You can skip school all together or devote your life to a PhD. Even if you do something that is almost exactly what your peers did, that last little bit that is different, even if slightly different, makes it your own. The experiences you have may be similar to someone else's, but how you respond and process them shapes you into who you are. It makes those experiences completely different for you.

End whatever experience you have with the plan to do better. That is what your early adult years teach you, not to handle financial stress or contemplate who you are as a person, but to simply go forth and do better.

PERFECTIONISM, LOVE, AND HAPPINESS: WHAT I REALLY LEARNED ON CAMPUS

~

The best thing I learned in my young-adult years is that perfectionism only exists within yourself. There isn't a perfect person out in the world, just a perfect decision for you to make. But that doesn't mean not making mistakes. It only means considering what makes your heart feel soft when making choices for you.

I learned what love feels like—not the connection you feel, but physically what it does to your body. It feels like electricity, lightning even, going down your spine—not merely the sparks you feel during a kiss, but sparks lighting up every inch of you. It isn't a metaphorical feeling. It's something others will notice, too. When the boy you love looks you in the eye and whispers, "you're on fire," he doesn't mean it literally but says it because your entire body feels hot; he can feel your whole body lighting up the same way you can.

Happiness is something I thought I fully understood. Sure, I didn't feel it all the time, but I understood it and could recognize it when it was there. Happiness is more complex than I thought but still very simple at the same time. Happiness isn't making your heart soft; rather, you know the happiness is coming when your heart goes soft.

People say that when making choices, do what makes you happy, but someone told me to do what made my heart *soft*, and that changed my life. I started paying attention to how my body felt and reacted to the choices presented to me. Did I want to run? Or did I feel safe and relaxed? That feeling of your body calming down, the relaxation, and peace is happiness. It is when your body lights up in a calm way. More of a slight glow than the sparks love brings.

I didn't think these were the things I would be learning at college. I thought I'd be learning about drinking games, walking home drunk, picking up guys, and whatever we covered in class. These experiences could have happened in other situations. I kissed a boy in the streets of Athens and thought I was in love only a few months prior to this experience, but experiencing true love and learning what happiness actually is are the things that mean I'll never regret the time I spent at Dartmouth.

So how does this affect life going forward? The big question is, is college a necessity? No, it is not a necessity. I truly believe that it isn't. I believe that the experiences I had were vital to me becoming the person I am, but also vital to every other human being. I'm not talking about frat parties and weird campus traditions. I'm talking about learning what love, happiness, and perfection actually are. Those are the vital lessons that I will carry with me for the rest of my life. I believe that they could have happened in other situations outside of college, but I think the thing that college did that allowed me to have them was force me to stay in one place. When things didn't work out for me in other places, I was able to pack up and start over again somewhere new. If I decide to stay somewhere, I could still start over with a new friend group, but college put every mistake I made on full display. Everybody knew my business, like in high school, but they were slightly more mature and able to process things better than high schoolers did. I think college forces people to grow up a tiny bit quicker—not fully grow up, but mature just enough to be able to handle being away from the people who raised you. That tiny bit of growth, that independence, makes a huge difference in how these young adults process things. Even though there were so many moments that felt way too much like high school, there were plenty more moments that showed me that it was way different.

What I began to wonder toward the end of this crazy experience was if that amount of growth these eighteen-year-olds were forced to go through so quickly was supposed to be a quick thing. I'm grateful I had the experience of being a college student for a bit, but this all happened in five months. I can't imagine going through even more over the course of four years, at least not in that type of context.

I believe that those moments in Athens and London should have been the ones where I learned love and happiness. Maybe it's because I look at my life like some kind of magical movie and a location like a fraternity just doesn't cut it for my dreamy outlook on life. I really believe that the magic of seeing the world intensifies those lessons we all learn as young adults. I guess that's because I have a love for travel. We must understand that everyone has different preferences in life. Someone might honestly feel more at home in a frat than in a hostel in Europe. So, this idea that everyone should follow this college path isn't a good idea. The ones that want to spend their twenties in Europe should, but those who feel safe at a college have every right to spend their time there.

College may have multiple paths for different degrees, but that doesn't make it a path with endless options. It still manages to limit people's options by restricting classes they can take or programs they can transfer into based on what college you go to. There are not endless doors in a college, and until we recognize that, we will continue to create generations of people who view their time in frat basements as their peak in life and look back wondering what all they could have done if they had chosen a different path for those four years. If the average adult has ten jobs in a lifetime, how many of those require a degree? And of the ones that don't require a degree, how many of those people feel that was the best career they could have chosen? I bet those people would feel pretty great if they got started in the vocation they actually love a lot sooner and avoided the debt.

THE NO-DEGREE LIFE

~

fter this experience, I didn't feel lost at all. I began to really understand what I wanted out of life. I don't know if it was the feeling of completing all the classic young adult things or if it was learning those big life lessons, but I felt at peace and confident that I could dive into the things I wanted to do full force with certainty that they were the right choices for me and that I was ready to move forward.

My life sounds a bit crazy, a tad traumatic, but the truth is, I am so grateful for all the things that happened. It might seem shocking to talk about the many miscarriages, the sexual trauma, and everything in between, but when you look at the statistics, these things are happening all over the country to people you know. We just don't give people safe spaces to talk about it. College made me feel a little less alone and made talking about these awful, terrible things seem way more important. I needed all of this to heal, move on, become my whole self, and create my safe home life.

I returned to my old state of avoiding campus and being greatly annoyed by fraternity members. I still brought the babies on campus, but I chose new spots to hang out, specifically near the art sculpture behind Berry Library. It was a quiet spot, typically, except for one time when Dartmouth students decided to play frisbee right next to the babies. They were friendly and stressed how cute they thought the twins were but got a bit rude after I thanked them and said, "They aren't mine though, I can't take credit." I don't know what response they expected or wanted. I am still slightly confused as to why that upset the grad student, but after my time on campus, I learned I will never fully understand what goes on in Dartmouth students' minds. Usually, the only excitement behind the library during the pandemic was a few local teens skateboarding, which the babies found very entertaining.

The world's state in 2020 played a role in the way I was forced to slow down. I'm not a very patient person, but suddenly I had to not simply trust that things would work out, but wait for them to, and that was something I didn't usually do. Usually, I could get started on whatever project I was dreaming up.

There I was at nineteen years old, packing up my dead grandmother's belongings to move into her house and start this confident new life for myself. It felt very full circle being able to begin a new chapter in the home after someone else's had ended. It took a bit to get settled; lots of unpacking, weird work schedules, and tears as I processed all that I had been through the past four years. The trauma, the college experience, the travels, the love, and the losses.

I adopted a second dog, two cats, and six chickens. One cat tragically passed away, and I found myself processing loss in a different way than I had before. I was able to feel at peace much quicker and understand why things happened the way they did.

I wrote a book and got it published—a dream I didn't think would come true until well into my thirties or forties. I launched a doula training program at multiple colleges, even Ivy League schools, like Dartmouth. In doing so, I found my place in these schools. I wasn't ever meant to enroll in college, but I did have a purpose there. I was able to connect with professors all over the world to do research with. Research on things I truly care about, even more so after the classes I took at Dartmouth.

I processed the relationships I had and truly began to understand why I had such a desire to have a family on my own. I wanted a partner for selfish reasons, like wanting someone to grill for me while I sat in the hot tub. I didn't want someone to parent with or love forever, at least not when this experience wrapped up. I wanted a handy guy who would just do house projects for me or be there if my car broke down. It was the same reason I wished my dad lived close by. So, I took control of my health and saw a fertility specialist, picked a donor, and started the process of trying for a baby in July 2020.

Despite the swearing off of relationships, I ended up meeting someone. I thought the London boy showed me how I should be treated. Not even close. This boy woke up at 6 a.m. to get me breakfast the first night he slept over. He texted flower emojis when I was sad. He offered food and back rubs when I felt sick. He checked in and wanted to text me throughout the day, unlike a frat boy. He had the best characteristics of both boys I loved and none of the terrible ones of the worst relationships I had been in. He grilled for me, helped with house projects, supported my baby dreams, helped me when I had writer's block, and kissed me under the stars. He wasn't The One, but that boy, this life, this job, these dreams . . . that's what this pseudo-college experience brought. It brought all those things I knew I would one day have but just wasn't ready for. There was a desire to have that experience, so I did. It's not an experience everyone should have, but I recommend you go after those experiences you desire.

They say you develop the characteristics your parents lacked in order to protect yourself. I think that's true, but not only of parents, but also of anyone who influences us. I prioritized empathy, understanding, freedom, independence, ambition, and a pioneering attitude from a young age. You get to decide who you are, what's important to you, and how you live. We have so much more control over our lives than we think we do. Others' dreams are no less important because they're different from yours. That girl who chooses sorority life and settling down with a fellow classmate at twenty-six, living a white-picket-fence lifestyle isn't "basic;" she's doing what sets her soul on fire, the same way you should be! Find the beauty and value in being different and chasing different dreams than other people. Learn to ignore those who do not support your beautiful life and surround yourself with those who do.

I realized that valuing others opinions often resulted in me getting hurt, and I began to focus less on that and more on working with people who had similar opinions and whom I could collaborate with. The understanding of others' views never went away, but the prioritization of people who support me became a big thing for me. I stopped allowing people to walk all over me, tell me I'm too young when I voice my dreams, and tell me I am not allowed to have the things I want. The difference between WASP families and me is that I believe we all deserve love, happiness, and everything we want out of life and there is no reason why we shouldn't have it, but I don't expect it to be handed to me.

This experience opened my eyes to the need for more resources on campus and the lack of support for groups of people who aren't cis white males that fit the preppy boy stereotype. Watching signs get plastered around campus with "Justice 4 Maha" on them and hearing more about the sexual harassment lawsuits happening at Dartmouth, I was fired up. No school is perfect, but Dartmouth seemed a little further from it than most. Like I said, I'm grateful for the lessons I learned there, but how am I supposed to tell others to do better, like my prof said, when I'm not? I began doing what I know how to do: providing support for families and babies. I partnered with organizations to provide adoption support, local centers to teach newborn care and childbirth support classes for free, and even began working with a nonprofit that connects pregnant students all over the nation with resources. I truly believe that college students should feel no shame when they either start a family by surprise or choose to start a family young, and they should not feel threatened or like they are going to lose opportunities because they had a baby.

As I sit in my home, I look around. There is a 1934 Dartmouth banner on the wall that belonged to my great-grandfather and a Dartmouth banner I purchased from the Dartmouth Co-op. I have a purple fireplace because this home is mine, a beautiful greenhouse, all my animals, and a bedroom that has been turned into a nursery for the day I become a mother. My life is still messy and hectic. I still enjoy flirting with frat boys and having crushes on the types of guys who dress preppy, grill for me, and play with my dogs, but I have no desire to end up with them. I am content with where I am at in life, and I fully trust that things are, and always will, work out how they're meant to, even if how they're meant to isn't what I initially imagined.

I realized that the people giving advice on how I had plenty of time and needed to slow down probably sensed a bit of desire in me—desire to have these experiences. When I announced my decision to have a baby, they didn't have anything to say about me being too young. They didn't have anything to say at all. Maybe they didn't agree with my choice, but they kept their mouths shut. I don't need them to agree. We all have the freedom to choose different paths. That's the whole point of why I wrote this. Everyone who achieves greatness is a little bit odd and completely out of the ordinary. Look at Van Gogh and Frida Kahlo. They would never have conformed to the mold Dartmouth set for them.

You can have the college experience the way I did, or you can enroll and have it the way the Greek-life students did, or even avoid it altogether, but no matter what you choose, you are the only one who knows if that course was right for you. If it was right, you won't really care when people tell you that you are missing out. It'll work out as it should.

There will be traumas, obstacles, wonderful moments, terrifying experiences, memories full of love, and so much more, but I'll tell you this: I don't like the saying, "Tomorrow isn't guaranteed." That sounds too dark and sad. Instead, I started saying, "The light isn't green forever." I was stuck at a stoplight one day. A green light appeared, but the car in front of me wouldn't go. Traffic was bad, I was in a rush to get home, and my mom was on the phone when I shouted that saying. That's how it originated, in a road-rage fit I threw in rush-hour traffic. It's true, though: you may not have that opportunity forever, so if you really want it, take it.

I leave you now with the words of Professor Walton: "Go into the world and do good."

ABOUT THE AUTHOR

~

I am Jess Kimball, a birth and postpartum doula practicing in Vermont. I graduated high school at age sixteen and began devoting my life to chasing after what makes my soul feel on fire. Throughout my travels and work endeavors, I was constantly reminded of my decision to not go to college. I decided to have a "pseudo-college experience," experiencing the social parts and "vital experiences" without being an actual student. This opportunity allowed me to feel confident in all my choices with no doubts about my decisions. I began creating college doula programs, writing more and more, and focusing on my dream to have a baby. I am passionate about chasing after what feels right to me, and I believe everyone should do so. I do things that bring me joy: paddle boarding, baking, traveling the world, caring for my many animals, capturing moments with my camera, and surrounding myself with life and light. I do what makes my heart feel soft.